The Art of Poetry volume 11

OCR poetry anthology, conflict

With thanks for their contributions to James Browning, Matthew Curry and Neil Jones.

Published by Peripeteia Press Ltd.

First published July 2017

ISBN: 978-0-9954671-7-0

Peripeteia.webs.com

Contents

Introductions   4

How to analyse a poem   9

Writing Literature essays   12

Writing comparative essays   18

Writing about language, sound, form & structure   22

Nice to metre   29

14 ways of looking at a poem   31

William Blake, *A Poison Tree*   34

Mary Lamb, *Envy*   40

William Wordsworth, *Extract from The Prelude*   45

Lord Byron, *The Destruction of Sennacherib*   52

Emily Dickinson, *A Certain Slant of Light*   57

Thomas Hardy, *The Man He Killed*   65

Wilfred Owen, *Anthem for Doomed Youth*   69

Keith Douglas, *Vergissmeinnicht*   74

Denise Levertov, *What were they like?*   82

Gillian Clarke, *Lament*   88

Seamus Heaney, *Punishment*   94

John Agard, *Flag*   101

Jo Shapcott, *Phrase Book*   108

Imtiaz Dharker, *Honour Killing*   114

Sujata Bhatt, *Partition*   120

Revision activities   128

Glossary   132

Recommended reading   136

About the authors   137

General Introduction to the The Art of Poetry series

The philosopher Nietzsche described his work as 'the greatest gift that [mankind] has ever been given'. The Elizabethan poet Edmund Spenser hoped his epic, *The Faerie Queene,* would magically transform its readers into noblemen. In comparison, our aims for *The Art of Poetry* series of books are a little more modest. Fundamentally we aim to provide books that will be of maximum use to English students and their teachers. In our experience, few students read essays on poems, yet, whatever specification they are studying, they have to write analytical essays on poetry. So, we've offering some models, written in a lively, accessible and, we hope, engaging style. We believe that the essay as a form needs demonstrating and championing, especially as so many revision books for students present information in broken down note form.

For Volume 1 we chose canonical poems for several reasons: Firstly, they are simply great poems, well worth reading and studying; secondly, we chose poems from across time so that they sketch in outline major developments in English poetry, from the Elizabethan period up until the present day, so that the volume works as an introduction to poetry and poetry criticism. Our popular volumes 2-5 focused on poems set at A-level by the Edexcel and AQA boards respectively. Volumes 6 and 7 tackled AQA's GCSE anthology and volumes 9 and 10 Edexcel's and Eduqas's GCSE anthologies. In this current volume, we turn our focus again to GCSE, providing critical support for students reading poems from OCR's poetry anthology. In particular, we hope our book will inspire students to aim for the very highest grades.

Introduction to Volume 11, conflict

An adventure into what one apprehends

When writing about themes, students often simply state what they think is the major theme of a poem. As OCR has kindly arranged these poems into a thematic cluster, writing something like 'this is a poem about conflict' wouldn't earn any marks. Instead you need to explore what this poem says about conflict and how the poet says this. Sometimes readers also labour under a misconception about the nature of poetry, believing that poems have secret messages that, rather annoyingly, poets have hidden under deliberately obscure language. The task of the reader becomes to decode the obscure language and extract the buried message. Unsurprisingly, this misconception of poetry as a sort of fancy subcategory of fables makes readers wonder why poets go to all the irritating trouble of hiding their messages in the first place. If they had something to say, why didn't the poet just say it and save everyone a lot of unnecessary fuss and bother? Why couldn't Blake, for instance, have just said that suppressing your emotions is a bad idea?

The Romantic poet, John Keats's comment about distrusting poetry that has a 'palpable design' on the reader has been much quoted. For Keats, and many poets, a 'palpable design' is an aspect of rhetoric and particularly of propaganda. A poem is not just a piece of propaganda for a poet's ideas. As the modern poet, George Szirtes puts it, poems are not 'rhymed advertisements for the already formed views of poets'. Here's George discussing the issue in his blog [ttp://georgeszirtes.blogspot.co.uk/]: 'A proper poem has to be a surprise: no surprise for the poet no surprise for the reader, said Robert Frost and I think that he and Keats were essentially right. A proper poem should arise out of a naked unguarded experience that elicits surprise in the imagination by extending the consciousness in some way. Poetry is not what one knows but an adventure into what one apprehends.'

Most poems are not merely prettified presentations of a poet's settled views about a particular theme or issue; they are more like thought experiments or journeys of exploration and discovery. In other words, poetry, like all art, is equipment for thinking and feeling. So, instead of writing that 'poem x is about conflict' try to think more carefully through what is interesting or unusual or surprising about the poem's presentation of these subjects. Sometimes the nature of the conflict will be obvious, as in poems exploring wars, such as Owen's and Douglas'; at other times the type of conflict might be more unusual or crop up in an incongruous context. What, for example, is the conflict explored in the extract from Wordsworth's The Prelude?

Approach a poem with questions in mind: What does the poem have to say about its theme? What angle does the poet take; is the poem celebratory, mournful, exploratory? To what extent does the poem take up arms and argue for something and have a 'palpable design'? Is the attitude to the subject consistent or does it change? To what extent is the poem philosophical or emotional? Do we learn something new, does it change how we think or feel? How might the poem have extended our thinking about its subject?

It would be trite to conclude that all these various poems are merely telling us that conflict is a terrible thing and that peaceful relationships are central to a fulfilling life. Sometimes conflict might be internal, psychological, emotional and a necessary aspect of a process of resolving an issue. If you're faced with an injustice, like Dharker in *Honour Killing* or Heaney in *Punishment*, some conflict may be necessary to right a wrong. In some of the poems there may be several conflicts at work, subtle as well as more obvious ones. Conflict is also central to art; the 'agon' of protagonist and antagonist comes from the Greek word for 'conflict' or 'struggle'. Are there any poems in OCR's anthology celebrating conflict? Are there any unusual or counterintuitive manifestations of conflict? Conflict as a source of creative inspiration? Conflict as an expression of identity and even of love? Are the poems meditations on the nature of conflict or powerful expressions of the experience of fighting?

An adventure into what you apprehend is a great way to conceptualise a poem. And it's very productive too as a way to think about writing poetry criticism.

The Exam

Assessment of poetry comprises 25% of your marks for English Literature GCSE. In the exam you will have to answer one question split into two parts. In the first part you will be asked to compare one named poem you have studied from the OCR anthology with an unseen poem on the same theme. OCR recommends you spend 45 minutes on this task. In the second part you will be asked to choose a poem from the anthology and explore in detail how it presents its theme(s). This second task should take 25 minutes.

Here's a sample question provided by OCR:

a) Compare how these poems present the effect of war on people's lives.
   Consider:
   - Ideas and attitudes
   - Tone and atmosphere
   - The effects of language and structure
[The poems are *Anthem for Doomed Youth* from the anthology and the

7

unseen poem is one by John Agard.]

    b) Explore in detail one other poem from your anthology that presents lives transformed by conflict.

Sample questions, assessment criteria, past papers, exemplar material and so forth are available on OCR's website.

In terms of preparing for the first task, OCR says that 'students will also need to read poetry more widely related to their chosen theme'. Obviously your teachers will help find suitable material, but a really good place to start would be the anthologies produced by the other main examination boards, as these feature material pitched at the same level. The AQA and Edexcel boards both have clusters within their anthologies on the theme of conflict. Lists of the poems are available online and there are also critical guides in *The Art of Poetry* series [volumes 6 and 13] on these conflict poems.

How to analyse a poem [seen or unseen]

A list of ingredients, not a recipe

Firstly, what not to do: sometimes pupils have been so programmed to spot poetic features such as alliteration that they start analysis of a poem with close reading of these micro aspects of technique. This is never a good idea. A far better strategy is to begin by trying to develop an overall understanding of what you think the poem is about. While all these poems are obviously about relationships of some sort or other, the nature of these relationships vary widely what they have say about this topic is also highly varied. Once you've established the central concerns, you can delve into the poem's interior, examining its inner workings in the light of these. And you should be flexible enough to adapt, refine or even reject your initial thoughts in the light of your investigation. The essential thing is to make sure that whether you're discussing imagery or stanza form, sonic effects or syntax, enjambment or vocabulary, you always explore the significance of the feature in terms of meanings and effect.

Someone once compared texts to cakes. When you're presented with a cake the first thing you notice is what it looks like. Probably the next thing you'll do is taste it and find out if you like the flavour. This aesthetic experience will come first. Only later might you investigate the ingredients and how it was made. Adopting a uniform reading strategy is like a recipe; it sets out what you must, do step by step, in a predetermined order. This can be helpful, especially when you start reading and analysing poems. Hence in our first volume in *The Art of Poetry* series we explored each poem under the same subheadings of narrator, characters, imagery, patterns of sound, form & structure and contexts, and all our essays followed essentially the same direction. Of course, this is a reasonable strategy for reading poetry and will stand you in good stead. However, this present volume takes a different, more flexible approach, because this book is designed for students aiming for levels 7 to 9, or A to A* in old currency, and to reach the highest levels your work needs to be a bit more conceptual, critical and individual. Writing frames are useful for beginners, like stabilisers when you learn to ride a bike. But, if you wish to write top level essays you need to develop your own frames.

Read our essays and you'll find that they all include the same principle ingredients – detailed, 'fine-grained' reading of crucial elements of poetry, imagery, form, rhyme and so forth - but each essay starts in a different way and each one has a slightly different focus or weight of attention on the various aspects that make up a poem. Once you feel you have mastered the apprentice strategy of reading all poems in the same way, we strongly recommend you put this generic essay recipe approach to one side and move on to a new way of reading, an approach that can change depending on the nature of the poem you're reading.

Follow your nose

Having established what you think a poem is about - its theme and what is interesting about the poet's treatment of the theme [the conceptual bit] - rather than then working through a pre-set agenda, decide what you honestly think are the most interesting aspects of the poem and start analysing these closely. This way your response will be original [a key marker of a top band essay] and you'll be writing about material you find most interesting. In other words, you're foregrounding yourself as an individual, critical reader. These most interesting aspects might be ideas or technique based, or both.

Follow your own, informed instincts, trust in your own critical intelligence as a reader. If you're writing about material that genuinely interests you, your writing is likely to be interesting for the examiner too. And, obviously, take advice from your teacher too, use their expertise.

Because of the focus on sonic effects and imagery other aspects of poems are often overlooked by students. It is a rare student, for instance, who notices how punctuation works in a poem and who can write about it convincingly. Few students write about the contribution of the unshowy function words, such as pronouns, prepositions or conjunctions, yet these words are crucial to any text. Of course, it would be a highly risky strategy to focus your whole essay on a seemingly innocuous and incidental detail of a poem. But coming at things from an unusual angle is as important to writing great essays as it is to the production of great poetry.

So, in summary, when reading a poem for the first time, such as when doing an 'unseen' style question, have a check list in mind, but don't feel you must follow someone else's generic essay recipe. Don't feel that you must always start with a consideration of imagery if the poem you're analysing has, for instance, an eye-catching form. Consider the significance of major features, such as imagery, vocabulary, sonic patterns and form. Try to write about these aspects in terms of their contribution to themes and effects. But also follow your nose, find your own direction, seek out aspects that genuinely engage you and write about these.

The essays in this volume provide examples and we hope they will encourage you to go your own way, at least to some extent, and to make discoveries for yourself. No single essay could possibly cover everything that could be said about any one of these poems; aiming to create comprehensive essays like this would be utterly foolish. And we have not tried to do so. Nor are our essays meant to be models for exam essays – they're far too long for that. They do, however, illustrate the sort of conceptualised, critical and 'fine-grained' exploration demanded for top grades at GCSE and beyond. There's always more to be discovered, more to say, space in other words for you to develop some original reading of your own, space for you to write your own individual essay recipe.

Writing literature essays

The **Big** picture and the small

An essay itself can be a form of art. And writing a great essay takes time, skill and practice. And also expert advice. Study the two figures in the picture carefully and describe what you can see. Channel your inner Sherlock Holmes to add any deductions you are able to form about the image. Before reading what we have to say, write your description out as a prose paragraph. Probably you'll have written something along the following lines:

First off, the overall impression: this picture is very blurry. Probably this indicates that either this is a very poor quality reproduction, or that it is a copy of a very small detail from a much bigger image that has been magnified several times. The image shows a stocky man and a medium-sized dog, both orientated towards something to their left, which suggests there is some point of interest in that direction. From the man's rustic dress (smock, breeches, clog-like boots) the picture is either an old one or a modern one depicting the past. The man appears to be carrying a stick and there's maybe a bag on his back. From all of these details we can probably deduce that he's a peasant, maybe a farmer or a shepherd.

Now do the same thing for picture two. We have even less detail here and again the picture's blurry. Particularly without the benefit of colour it's hard to

determine what we're seeing other than a horizon and maybe the sky. We might just be able to make out that in the centre of the picture is the shape of the sun. From the reflection, we can deduce that the image is of the sun either setting or rising over water. If it is dawn this usually symbolises hope, birth and new beginnings; if the sun is setting it conventionally symbolises the opposite – the end of things, the coming of night/ darkness, death.

If you're a sophisticated reader, you might well start to think about links between the two images. Are they, perhaps, both details from the same single larger image, for instance.

Well, this image might be even harder to work out. Now we don't even have a

whole figure, just a leg, maybe, sticking up in the air. Whatever is happening here, it looks painful and we can't even see the top half of the body. From the upside orientation, we might guess that the figure is or has fallen. If we put this image with the one above, we might think the figure has fallen into water as there are horizontal marks on the image that could be splashes. From the quality of this image we can deduce that this is an even smaller detail blown-up.

You may be wondering by now why we've suddenly moved into rudimentary art appreciation. On the other hand, you may already have worked out the

point of this exercise. Either way, bear with us, because this is the last picture for you to describe and analyse. So, what have we here? Looks like another peasant, again from the past, perhaps medieval (?) from the smock-like dress, clog-like shoes and the britches. This character is also probably male and seems to be pushing some wooden apparatus from left to right. From the ridges at the bottom left of the image we can surmise that he's working the land, probably driving a plough. Noticeably the figure has his back

to us; we see his turned away from us, suggesting his whole concentration is on the task at hand. In the background appear to be sheep, which would fit with our impression that this is an image of farming. It seems likely that this image and the first one come from the same painting. They have a similar style and subject and it is possible that these sheep belong to our first character. This image is far less blurry than the other one. Either it is a better-quality reproduction, or this is a larger, more significant detail extracted from the original source. If this is a significant detail it's interesting that we cannot see the character's face. From this we can deduce that he's not important in and of himself; rather he's a representative figure and the important thing is what he is and what he isn't looking at.

Okay, we hope we haven't stretched your patience too far. What's the point of all this? Well, let's imagine we prefixed the paragraphs above with an introduction, along the following lines: 'The painter makes this picture interesting and powerful by using several key techniques and details' and that we added a conclusion, along the lines of 'So now I have shown how the painter has made this picture interesting and powerful through the use of a number of key techniques and details'. Finally, substitute painter and picture for writer and text. If we put together our paragraphs into an essay what would be its strengths and weaknesses? What might be a better way of writing our essay?

Consider the strengths first off. The best bits of our essay, we humbly suggest, are the bits where we begin to explain what we are seeing, when we do the Holmes like deductive thinking. Another strength might be that we have started to make links between the various images, or parts of a larger image, to see how they work together to provide us more information. A corresponding weakness is that each of our paragraphs seems like a separate chunk of writing. The weaker parts of the paragraphs are where we simply describe what we can see. More importantly though, if we used our comments on image one as our first paragraph we seem to have started in a rather random way. Why should we have begun our essay with that image? What was the logic behind that? And most importantly of all, if this image is an analogue for a specific aspect of a text, such as a poem's imagery or a novel's dialogue we have dived straight into to analysing this technical aspect before we're established any overall sense of the painting/ text. And this is a very common fault with GCSE English Literature essays. As we've said before and will keep saying, pupils start writing detailed micro-analysis of a detail such as alliteration before they have established the big picture of what the text is about and what the answer to the question they've been set might be. Without this big picture it's very difficult to write about the significance of the micro details. And the major marks for English essays are reserved for explanations of the significance and effects generated by a writer's craft.

Now we'll try a different and much better approach. Let's start off with the big picture, the whole image. The painting on the next page is called *Landscape with the fall of Icarus*. It's usually attributed to the Renaissance artist, Pieter Breughel and was probably painted in the 1560s. Icarus is a character from

 Greek mythology. He was the son of the brilliant inventor, Daedalus. Trapped on Crete by the evil King Minos, Daedalus and Icarus managed to escape when the inventor created pairs of giant feathered wings. Before they took to sky Daedalus warned his son not to get too excited and fly too near the sun as the wings were held together by wax that might melt. Icarus didn't listen, however. The eventual result was that he plummeted back to earth, into the sea more precisely and was killed.

Applying this contextual knowledge to the painting we can see that the image is about how marginal Icarus' tragedy is in the big picture. Conventionally we'd expect any image depicting such a famous myth to make Icarus's fall the dramatic centre of attention. The main objects of this painting, however, are emphatically not the falling boy hitting the water. Instead our eye is drawn to the peasant in the centre of the painting, pushing his plough (even more so in colour as his shirt is the only red object in an otherwise greeny-yellow landscape) and the stately galleon sailing calmly past those protruding legs. Seeing the whole image, we can appreciate the significance of the shepherd and the ploughman looking up and down and to the left. The point being made is how they don't even notice the tragedy because they have work to do and need to get on with their lives. The animals too seem unconcerned. As W. H. Auden puts it, in lines from *Musée des Beaux Arts*, 'everything turns away /

Quite leisurely from the disaster'.

To sum up, when writing an essay on any literary text do not begin with close-up analysis of micro-details. Begin instead with establishing the whole picture: What the text is about, what key techniques the writer uses, when it was written, what sort of text it is, what effects it has on the reader. Then, when you zoom in to examine smaller details, such as imagery, individual words, metre or sonic techniques you can discuss these in relation to their significance in terms of this bigger picture.

What would our art appreciation essay look like now?

Paragraph #1: Introduction – myth of Icarus, date of painting, the way our eyes is drawn away from his tragic death to much more ordinary life going around him. Significance of this – even tragic suffering goes on around us without us even noticing, we're too busy getting on with our lives.

Paragraph #2: We could, of course, start with our first figure and follow the same order as we've presented the images here. But wouldn't it make more logical sense to discuss first the biggest, more prominent images in the painting first? So, our first paragraph is about the ploughman and his horse. How his figure placed centrally and is bent downwards towards the ground and turned left away from us etc.

Paragraph #3: The next most prominent image is the ship. Also moving from right to left, as if the main point of interest in the painting is off in that direction. Here we could consider the other human agricultural figure, the shepherd and his dog and, of course, the equally oblivious sheep.

Paragraph #4: Having moved on to examining background details in the painting we could discuss the symbolism of the sun on the horizon. While this could be the sun rising, the context of the story suggests it is more likely to be setting. The pun of the sun/son going down makes sense.

Paragraph #5: Finally, we can turn our attention to the major historical and literary figure in this painting, Icarus and how he is presented. This is the key image in terms of understanding the painting's purpose and effect.

Paragraph #6: Conclusion. What is surprising about this picture. How do the choices the painter makes affect us as viewer/ reader? Does this painting make Icarus's story seem more pathetic, more tragic or something else?

Now, all you have to do is switch from a painting to a poem.

Big pictures, big cakes, recipes and lists of instructions; following your own nose and going your own way. Whatever metaphors we use, your task is to bring something personal and individual to your critical reading of poems and to your essay writing.

Writing comparative essays

The following is adapted from our discussion of this topic in *The Art of Writing English Literature Essay*s A-level course companion, and is a briefer version, tailored to the GCSE exam task. Fundamentally comparative essays want you to display not only your ability to intelligently talk about literary texts, but also your ability to make meaningful connections between them. The first starting point is your topic. This must be broad enough to allow substantial thematic overlapping of the texts. However, too little overlap and it will be difficult to connect the texts; too much overlap and your discussion will be lopsided and one-dimensional. In the case of the GCSE exam, the broad topic will be conflict, but this may be broken down into various sub-themes, such as the effects of conflict or conflict within the mind. The exam question will ask you to focus on the methods used by the poets to explore how two poems present one of these themes. You will also be directed to write specifically on language and imagery and tone and atmosphere.

One poem from the anthology will be specified and printed on the paper. You will have to compare and contrast this with a poem you haven't seen before. You could prepare for this tricky question beforehand by matching up each of your OCR anthology poems with other poems on the theme of conflict. As we've already suggested, a good source of these are the anthologies produced by the other examination boards. Obviously planning and writing comparative essays is also essential practice.

Grasping how best to write comparative essays is also key to your chances of reaching the top grades. The very best comparative essays actually find that what seemed like clear similarities become subtle differences and vice versa while still managing to find rock solid similarities to build their foundations on. Check the mark scheme for this question and you'll notice that to reach the top grade your comparison must be 'well-structured'. How should you structure a comparative essay? Consider the following alternatives. Which one is best and why?

Essay Structure #1

1. Introduction
2. Main body paragraph #1 - Text A
3. Main body paragraph #2 - Text A
4. Main body paragraph #3 - Text B
5. Main body paragraph #4 - Text B
6. Conclusion

Essay Structure #2

1. Introduction
2. Main body paragraph #1 - Text A
3. Main body paragraph #2 - Text A
4. Main body paragraph #3 - Text B
5. Main body paragraph #4 - Text B
6. Comparison of main body paragraphs #1 & #3 - Text A + B
7. Comparison of main body paragraphs #2 & #4 - Text A + B
8. Conclusion

Essay Structure #3

1. Introduction
2. Main body paragraph #1 - Text A + B
3. Main body paragraph #2 - Text A + B
4. Main body paragraph #3 - Text A + B
5. Main body paragraph #4 - Text A + B
6. Conclusion

We hope you will agree that 3 is the optimum option. Option 1 is the dreaded 'here is everything I know about text A, followed by everything I know by Text B' approach where the examiner has to work out what the connections are between the texts. This will score the lowest marks. Option 2 is better: There is some attempt to compare the two texts. However, it is a very inefficient way of comparing the two texts. For comparative essay writing the most important thing is to discuss both texts together. This is the most effective and efficient way of achieving your overall aim. Option 3 does this by comparing and contrasting the two texts under common umbrella headings. This naturally encourages comparison. Using comparative discourse markers, such as 'similarly', 'in contrast to', 'conversely' 'likewise' and 'however', also facilitates effective comparison.

When writing about each poem, make sure you do not work chronologically through it, summarising the content of each stanza. Responses of this sort typically start with 'In the first stanza' and employ discourse markers of time rather than comparison, such as 'after', 'next', 'then' and so forth. Even if your reading is analytical rather than summative, your essay should not work through the poem from the opening to the ending. Instead you could use OCR's bullet points to structure your essay, so that your first paragraphs explore what these two poems tell us about conflict, your second section explores tone and atmosphere and your last section of your essay discusses language and structure. There's nothing wrong with this approach and it will serve you well for most of the poems. However, as we've already advised, you should be prepared to be flexible with your approach and your essay structure. If you've little to say about tone, for instance, but have lots of great points about language or structure, or if you're particularly struck by the writer's choices of vocabulary, be confident enough to foreground these aspects in your essay and write about them in more detail. In the end examiners will reward intelligent, well informed analysis of ideas and techniques and perceptive comparison of texts.

> what do those two poems tell us about
  conflict
> tone and atmosphere
> language & structure

Writing about language

Poems are paintings as well as windows; we look at them as well as through them. As you know, special attention should be paid to language in poetry because of all the literary art forms poetry, in particular, employs language in a precise, self-conscious and distinctive way. Ideally in poetry, every word should count. Analysis of language falls into distinct categories:

- By diction we mean the vocabulary used in a poem. A poem might be composed from the ordinary language of everyday speech or it might use elaborate, technical or elevated phrasing. Or both. At one time, some words and types of words were considered inappropriate for the rarefied field of poetry. The great Irish poet, W. B. Yeats never referred to modern technology in his poetry, there are no cars, or tractors or telephones, because he did not consider such things fitting for poetry. When much later, Philip Larkin used swear words in his otherwise well-mannered verse the effect was deeply shocking. Modern poets have pretty much dispensed with the idea of there being an elevated literary language appropriate for poetry. Hence in the OCR anthology you'll find all sorts of modern, everyday language.

- Grammatically a poem may use complex or simple sentences [the key to which is the conjunctions]; it might employ a wash of adjectives and adverbs, or it may rely extensively on the bare force of nouns and verbs. Picking out and exploring words from specific grammatical classes has the merit of being both incisive and usually illuminating.

- Poets might mix together different types, conventions and registers of language, moving, for example, between formal and informal, spoken and written, modern and archaic, and so forth. Arranging the diction in the poem in terms of lexico-semantic fields, by register or by etymology, helps reveal underlying patterns of meaning.

- For almost all poems imagery is a crucial aspect of language. Broadly imagery is a synonym for description and can be broken down into two types, sensory and figurative. Sensory imagery means the words and phrases that appeal to our senses, to touch and taste, hearing, smell and sight. Sensory imagery is evocative; it helps to take us into the world of the poem to share the experience being described. Figurative imagery, in particular, is always significant. As we have mentioned, not all poems rely on metaphors and similes; these devices are only part of a poet's box of tricks, but figurative language is always important when it occurs because it compresses multiple meanings into itself. To use a technical term figurative images are polysemic - they contain many meanings. Try writing out the all the meanings contained in a metaphor in a more concise and economical way. Even simple, everyday metaphors compress meaning. If we want to say our teacher is fierce and powerful and that we fear his or her wrath, we can more concisely say our teacher is a dragon.

Writing about patterns of sound

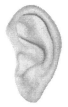 Like painters, some poets have powerful visual imaginations, while other poets have stronger auditory imaginations are more like musicians. And some poems are like paintings, others are more like pieces of music.

Firstly, what not to do: Tempting as it may be to spot sonic features of a poem and list these, don't do this. Avoid something along the lines of 'The poet uses alliteration here and the rhyme scheme is ABABCDCDEFEFGG'. Sometimes, indeed, it may be tempting to set out the poem's whole rhyme scheme like this. Resist the temptation: This sort of identification of features is worth zero marks. Marks in exams are reserved for attempts to link techniques to meanings and to effects.

Probably many of us have been sitting in English lessons listening somewhat sceptically as our English teacher explains the surprisingly specific significance of a seemingly random piece of alliteration in a poem. Something along the lines 'The double d sounds here reinforce a sense of invincible strength' or 'the harsh repetition of the 't' sounds suggests anger'. Through all our minds at some point may have passed the idea that, in these instances, English teachers appear to be using some sort of Enigma-style secret symbolic decoding machine that reveals how particular patterns of sounds have such definite encoded meanings.

And this sort of thing is not all nonsense. Originally deriving from an oral tradition, poems are, of course, written for the ear as much as for the eye, to be heard as much as read. A poem is a soundscape as much as it is a set of meanings. Sounds are, however, difficult to tie to very definite meanings and effects. By way of example, the old BBC Radiophonic workshop, which produced ambient sounds for radio and television programmes, used the same sounds in different contexts, knowing that the audience would perceive them in the appropriate way because of that context. Hence the sound of bacon sizzling, of an audience clapping and of feet walking over gravel were actually recordings of an identical sound. Listeners heard them differently because of the context. So, we may, indeed, be able to spot the repeated 's' sounds in a poem, but whether this creates a hissing sound, yes like a snake, or the susurration of the sea will depend on the context within the poem and the ears of the reader. Whether a sound is soft and soothing or harsh and grating is also open to interpretation.

The idea of connecting these sounds to meanings or significance is a productive one. And your analysis will be most convincing if you use several pieces of evidence together. In other words, rather than try to pick out individual examples of sonic effects we recommend you explore the weave or pattern of sounds, the effects these generate and their contribution to feelings and ideas. For example, this might mean examining how alliteration and assonance are used together to achieve a particular mimetic effect.

Writing about form & structure

As you know, there are no marks for simply identifying textual features. This holds true for language, sounds and also for form. Consider instead the relationship between a poem's form and its content, themes and effects. Form is not merely decorative or ornamental: A poem's meanings and effects are generated through the interplay of form and content. Broadly speaking the form can either work with or against a poem's content. Conventionally a sonnet, for instance, is about love, whereas a limerick is a comic form. A serious love poem in the form of a limerick would be unusual, as would a sonnet about an old man with a beard.

Sometimes poetic form can create an ironic backdrop to highlight an aspect of content. An example would be a formally elegant poem about something  monstrous, or a fragile form containing something robust. Owen's use of the sonnet in *Anthem for Doomed Youth* might spring to mind. The artist Grayson Perry uses form in this ironic way. Rather than depicting the sort of picturesque, idealised images we expect of ceramics, Perry's pots and urns depict modern life in bright, garish colours. The urn pictured, for instance, is entitled *Modern Family* and depicts two gay men with a boy who they have presumably adopted. A thrash metal concert inside a church, a philosophical essay via text message, a fine crystal goblet filled with cherryade would be further examples of ironic relationships between message and medium, content and context or form.

****

Reading form

Put a poem before your eyes. Start off taking a panoramic perspective: Think of the forest, not the trees. Perhaps mist over your eyes a bit. Don't even read the words, just look at the poem, like at a painting. Is the poem slight, thin, fat, long, short? What is the relation of whiteness to blackness? Why might the poet have chosen this shape? Does it look regular or irregular? A poem about a long winding river will probably look rather different from one about a small pebble, or should do. Unless form is being employed ironically. Now read the poem a couple of times. First time, fast as you can, second time more slowly and carefully. How does the visual layout of the poem relate to what it seems to be about? Does this form support, or create a tension against, the content? Is the form one you recognise, like a sonnet, or is it more open, more irregular like free verse? Usually the latter is obvious from the irregularity of the stanzas, line lengths and lack of metre or rhyme.

As Hurley and O'Neill explain in *Poetic Form: An Introduction*, like genre, form sets expectations: 'In choosing form, poets bring into play associations and expectations which they may then satisfy, modify or subvert'.[1] We've already suggested that if we see a poem is a sonnet or a limerick this recognition will set up expectations about the nature of the poem's content. The same thing works on a smaller level; once we have noticed that a poem's first stanza is a quatrain, we expect it to continue in this neat, orderly fashion. If the quatrain's rhyme scheme is xaxa, xbxb, in which only the second and fourth lines rhyme, we reasonably expect that the next stanza will be xcxc. So, if it isn't we need to consider why.

After taking in the big picture in terms of choice of form in relation to content zoom in: Explore the stanza form, lineation, punctuation, the use of enjambment and caesura. Single line stanzas draw attention to themselves. If they are end-stopped they can suggest isolation, separation. Couplets imply twoness. Stanzas of three lines are called tercets and feature in villanelles and terza rima. On the page, both these forms tend to look rather delicate, especially if separated from each other by the silence of white space. Often balanced through rhyme, quatrains look a bit more robust and sturdy. Cinquains are swollen quatrains in which the last line often seems to throw

---

[1] Hurley & O'Neill, *Poetic Form, An Introduction*, p.3

the stanza out of balance.

Focus in on specific examples and on points of transition. For instance, if a poem has four regular quatrains followed by a couplet, examine the effect of this change. If we've been ticking along nicely in iambic metre and suddenly trip on a trochee, examine why. Consider regularity. Closed forms of poems, such as sonnets, are highly regular with set rhyme schemes, metre and number of lines. The opposite form is called 'open', the most extreme version of which is free verse. In free verse poems, the poet dispenses with any set metre, rhyme scheme or recognisable traditional form. What stops this sort of poetry from being prose chopped up to look like verse? The care of the design on the page. Hence, we need to focus here on lineation. Enjambment runs over lines and makes connections; caesura pauses a line and separates words. Lots of enjambment generates a sense of the language running away from the speaker. Lots of caesuras generate a halting, hesitant, choppy movement to lines. Opposites, these devices work in tandem and where they fall is always significant in a good poem.

Remember poetic form is never merely decorative. And bear in mind too the fact that the most volatile materials require the strongest containers.

Nice to metre...

A brief guide to metre and rhythm in poetry

Why express yourself in poetry? Why read words dressed up and expressed as a poem? What can you get from poetry that you can't from prose? There are many compelling answers to these questions. Here, though, we're going to concentrate on one aspect of the unique appeal of poetry – the structure of sound in poetry. Whatever our stage of education, we are all already sophisticated at detecting and using structured sound. Try reading the following sentences without any variation whatsoever in how each sound is  emphasised, and they will quickly lose what essential human characteristics they have. The sentences will sound robotic. So, in a sense, we won't be teaching anything new here. It's just that in poetry the structure of sound is carefully unusually crafted and created. It becomes a key part of what a poem is.

We will introduce a few new key technical terms along the way, but the ideas are straightforward. Individual sounds [syllables] are either stressed [emphasised, sounding louder and longer] or unstressed. As well as clustering into words and sentences for meaning, these sounds [syllables] cluster into rhythmic groups or feet, producing the poem's metre, which is the characteristic way its rhythm works.

In some poems, the rhythm is very regular and may even have a name, such as iambic pentameter. At the other extreme a poem may have no discernible regularity at all. As we have said, this is called free verse. It is vital to remember that the sound in a good poem is structured so that it combines effectively with the meanings.

For example, take a look at these two lines from Marvell's *To his Coy Mistress*:

'But at my back I alwaies hear
Times winged Chariot hurrying near:'

Forgetting the rhythms for a moment, Marvell is basically saying at this point 'Life is short, Time flies, and it's after us'. Now concentrate on the rhythm of his words.

- In the first line every other syllable is stressed: 'at', 'back', 'al', 'hear'.
- Each syllable before these is unstressed 'But', 'my', 'I', 'aies'.
- This is a regular beat or rhythm which we could write
  ti TUM / ti TUM / ti TUM / ti TUM , with the / separating the feet. ['Feet' is the technical term for metrical units of sound]
- This type of two beat metrical pattern is called iambic, and because there are four feet in the line, it is tetrameter. So this line is in 'iambic tetrameter'. [Tetra is Greek for four]
- Notice that 'my' and 'I' being unstressed diminishes the speaker, and we are already prepared for what is at his 'back', what he can 'hear' to be bigger than him, since these sounds are stressed.
- On the next line, the iambic rhythm is immediately broken off, since the next line hits us with two consecutive stressed syllables straight off: 'Times' 'wing'. Because a pattern had been established, when it suddenly changes the reader feels it, the words feel crammed together more urgently, the beats of the rhythm are closer, some little parcels of time have gone missing.

A physical rhythmic sensation is created of time slipping away, running out. This subtle sensation is enhanced by the stress-unstress-unstress pattern of words that follow, 'chariot hurrying' [TUM-ti-ti, TUM-ti-ti]. So the hurrying sounds underscore the meaning of the words.

14 ways of looking at a poem

Though conceived as pre-reading exercises, most of these tasks work just as well for revision.

1. Mash them (1) – mix together lines from two or more poems. The students' task is to untangle the poems from each other.

2. Mash them (2) – the second time round make the task significantly harder. Rather than just mixing whole lines, mash the poems together more thoroughly, words, phrases, images and all, so that unmashing seems impossible. At first sight.

3. Dock the last stanza or few lines from a poem. The students should come up with their own endings for the poem. Compare with the poet's version. Or present the poem without its title. Can the students come up with a suitable one?

4. Break a poem into segments. Split the class into groups. Each group work in isolation on their segment and feedback on what they discover. Then their task is to fit the poem and their ideas about it together as a whole.

5. Give the class the first and last stanza of a poem. Their task is to provide the filling. They can choose to attempt the task at beginner level (in prose) or at world class level (in poetry).

6. Add superfluous words to a poem. Start off with obvious interventions, such as the interjection of blatantly alien, noticeable words. Try smuggling 'pineapple', 'bourbon' and 'haberdashers' into any of the poems and see if you can get it past the critical sensors.

7. Repeat the exercise – This time using much less extravagant words. Try to smuggle in a few intensifiers, such as 'really', 'very' and 'so'. Or extra adjectives.

8. Collapse the lineation in a poem and present it as continuous prose. The students' task is to put it back into verse. Discussing the various pros and cons or various possible arrangements – short lines, long lines, irregular lines - can be very productive. Pay particular attention to line breaks and the words that end them. After a whatever-time-you-deem-fit, give the class the pattern of the first stanza. They then have to decide how to arrange the next stanza. Drip feed the rest of the poem to them.

9. Find a way to present the shapes of each poem on the page without the words. The class should work through each poem, two minutes at a time, speculating on what the shape might tell us about the content of the poem. This exercise works especially well as a starter activity. We recommend you use two poems at a time, as the comparison helps students to recognise and appreciate different shapes.

10. Test the thesis that an astute reader can recognise poems by men from those written by women. Give the class one of the poems, such as *A Poison Tree* or *Lament*, without the name of the poet. Ask them to identify whether the writer is male or female and to explain their reasons for identifying them as such. Try again with another poem.

11. Split the class into groups. Each group should focus their analysis on a different feature of the poem. Start with the less obvious aspects: Group 1 should concentrate on enjambment and caesuras; group 2 on punctuation; group 3 on the metre and rhythm; group 4 on function words – conjunctions, articles, prepositions. 2-5 mins. only. Then swap focus, four times. Share findings.

12. In *Observations on Poetry*, Robert Graves wrote that 'rhymes properly used are the good servants whose presence at the dinner-table gives the guests a sense of opulent security; never awkward or over-clever, they hand the dishes silently and professionally. You can trust them not to interrupt the conversation or allow their personal disagreements to come to the notice of the guests; but some of them are getting very old for their work'. Explore the poets' use of rhyme in the light of Graves' comment. Are the rhymes ostentatiously original or old hat? Do they stick out of the poem or are they neatly tucked in? Are they dutiful servants of meaning or noisy disrupters of the peace?

13. The Romantic poet, John Keats, claimed that 'we hate poetry that has a palpable design upon us – and if we do not agree seems to put its hand its breeches pock'. Apply his comment to this selection of poems. Do any seem to have a 'palpable design' on the reader? If so, how does the poet want us to respond?

14. Each student should crunch the poem down to one word per line. Discuss this process as a class. Project the poem so the whole class can see it and start the crunching process by indicating and then crossing-out the function words from each line. Now discuss which of the remaining words is most important. This will also give you an opportunity to refer to grammatical terms, such as nouns and verbs. Once each line has been reduced to one word, from this list, pupils should crunch again. This time all that should remain are the five most important words in the whole poem. Now they need to write two or three sentences for each of these words explaining exactly why they are so important and why the poet didn't choose any of the possible synonyms.

'Tell all the Truth but tell it slant'

EMILY DICKINSON

The Author & Printer W Blake

William Blake, *A Poison Tree*

A fool sees not the same tree that a wise man sees

Let's be frank, this is a very simple poem, is it not? A young child could read and understand it pretty easily and quickly. Look, for instance, at the diction. There's not a word in this poem over two syllables long and most are monosyllables, nor are there any words that'd be unfamiliar to most Year Seven pupils. Perhaps only 'deceitful' or 'wrath' would cause any problems at all. Simplicity of vocabulary is mirrored by structural simplicity. The construction of the sentences, for example, is very basic. Mostly they follow the simplest possible sentence pattern; the subject at the start 'I', followed by a simple verb, e.g. 'was' and a common adjective, such as 'angry' and then an object, e.g. 'my friend'. These rudimentary sentences are also arranged together using the simplest possible connection, the conjunction 'and'. Technically, grammatically, sentences connected by 'and' are called 'co-ordinating' sentences, as opposed to subordinating ones, and technically, grammatically it makes them all simple sentences. This highlights the lack of explanation for the actions depicted in the poem; the speaker concentrates on telling us, seemingly very straightforwardly, rather starkly, their story without any more complex reflection or commentary on its significance. That is left for us, the readers, to supply.

If we strip the poem right down to its bare skeleton its very simple structure becomes even more apparent; 'I was angry, I told, and I, and I, and with, and it, Till it, and my, and he, and into, when.' Only two subordinating conjunctions are utilised to tell the whole narrative, 'til' and 'when'. This pattern sounds very much like a child telling a story, an over-excited child, perhaps, letting the words come out in a rush, 'and I, and then he, and then I'. Check the stories you wrote early in your school career and possibly your teachers will have advised you to vary your sentences by not connecting them all with an 'and then'. So, can we surmise from the extreme simplicity of diction, syntax and sentence construction that the speaker of Blake's poem is a child?

The form of the poem is also simple. Familiar looking quatrains with a couplet rhyme scheme and consistently full rhymes. Nothing here to spook the reader or give us too much to tax our brains. What of the narrative the poem tells?

Perhaps this might be a bit more complex. Well, not really. First off, the story feels kind of familiar. That tempting 'apple bright', the 'foe', the theft and the punishment have a fairy tale quality, the sort of story we associate with childhood. We might, for instance, think of *Snow White*. It also reads like a parable, a simple illustration of a moral truth. It seems too to allude to another temptation story, perhaps the most famous and seminal one in Western culture, the story of the temptation and fall of Adam and Eve. So, again, the familiarity of the basic outline of the story, like the diction, the syntax and the grammar make the poem easy to read and understand. And yet. If we think for a moment of the allusion to the Adam and Eve story some of the complexity of

A Poisoned Tree begins to come into focus. Because in the Biblical narrative of Genesis it's God who places the delicious, but expressly forbidden, fruit in the Garden of Eden. And God's foe is not Adam and Eve, but Satan, the rebel angel disguised as a snake who will perform the role of tempter. And God's motivation for setting up the temptation of Adam and Eve was to allow them free will and to orchestrate man's eventual redemption by the sacrifice of his son, Jesus Christ. The speaker of Blake's poem, who places the tempting 'apple bright' into his 'garden' does not, however, do this for moral reasons or for the eventual betterment of humankind; rather he, she or its actions are fired by anger and developed through cunning, 'deceitful wiles'. Is, God, in fact the narrator of Blake's poem? Apply this literary/ religious context to the poem and quite suddenly everything about A Poison Tree is revealed to be much more complex than we might have first thought.

Unacted Desires

Seemingly small changes often have enormous consequences in Blake's poetry and so it is with this poem from Songs of Experience [1793]. The opening sentences mirror each other, except for a few crucial words. In the first example the anger is expressed or released and the issue apparently resolved. In the second example, the anger is not expressed and grows stronger as a result. It seems the speaker deliberately nurtures his anger, encourages it to grow more potent;

he 'watered' and 'sunned' it like a plant. Crucially, the unexpressed anger remains inside the speaker and mutates like some sort of dangerous alien, while inside him. Modern psychologists would call this repression; by not being expressed the anger is buried in the speaker's subconscious mind where it develops and grows. In other words, Blake's simple-seeming parable appears to anticipate the sort of insights into the workings of the mind the academic discipline of Psychology would taxonomise over a hundred years after the poet's death! And the extensive use of symbolism in the poem fits with this reading too, as symbolic language is the language of the subconscious working of the mind - the language of dreams. Not such a simple poem, after all.

In Romantic poetry following one's heart usually leads to making good moral decisions. On the other hand, ignoring strong feelings and the heart's desires in Romantic poetry usually ends badly. These tendencies in Romantic Literature as a whole are found write large and in bold in Blake's work. He was the poet who wrote, 'He who desires but acts not breeds pestilence'. If you think that's pretty strong, how about this: 'sooner murder an infant in its cradle than nurse unacted desires'! Even taking the rhetorical hyperbole into account, that's quite a thing to say. So, not following your feelings leads to pestilence and is worse than murdering a baby.

So, what do these insights tell us about the poem? Firstly, that the simplicity is only a superficial matter of style. The poem's limpid surface presents itself as simple, but A Poison Tree actually has great, hidden depths. We might have realised this from Blake's use of symbols, as symbols always concentrate multiple interpretations, or from his troubling re-working of temptation stories. But what do our psychological insights reveal about the 'moral' or the 'message' of the poem? Now, not all poems have a moral or message, but this one appears to be set up like a parable to guide the reader in some way. We've already been alerted to the dangers of mistaking the surface for the whole poem, and  we know that Blake wrote that fools and wise men do not see the same tree. What did he mean by that exactly? Surely that though both the fool and the wise man see the 'same tree' they see it in different ways. In other words, the tree doesn't change it's the perception of the viewer/reader that changes, and changes everything. In other words, we've been warned off the sort of simplistic, foolish reading this essay opened with. To read the poem that way is to read like a fool. But, nevertheless, the narrative does seem straightforward. The narrator felt anger, didn't say anything, allowed it to build up inside him, created a trap for his enemy and the story ends triumphantly with the foe poleaxed by his theft of the poisoned fruit. A decisive 1-0 to the narrator, we might think. But, we'd foolish to think like that. Because it isn't just the foe that is poleaxed at the end of this poem, so too is the narrator, but in a subtler psychological and moral sense.

The narrator begins the story as an innocent, telling us in simple detail about their uncomplicated psychology and actions. However, the repression of their anger in the fourth line breeds pestilence *inside* the narrator. The inverted anger has a corrupting effect on its host. Soon he/she/it is smiling falsely and employing 'soft deceitful wiles' to trick their adversary. [In passing, that surprising adjective to describe deceit is a brilliant touch. Firstly, it makes an abstract idea concrete, in this case turning deceit into something we can touch. Secondly the tactile softness suggests the attractiveness of the deceit to speaker and his 'foe'. Lastly it is itself a misleading word to apply to this idea - deceit is rarely 'soft'; hence it enacts deceit]. It's a small step from feeling anger to the sadistic satisfaction expressed in the last lines of the poem:

'In the morning glad I see
My foe outstretched beneath the tree'

So the narrator has become a murderer. And it was a swift step; it all happened so fast, in just four short stanzas. Didn't that punishment seem even a little bit disproportionate to the narrator, a little excessive? If not, why not?

38

Double vision

Blake's poem is like a gestalt picture. It can be seen from different perspectives at the same time. For the narrator of the poem perhaps the story seems to have turned out rather well. They won, didn't they? At a deeper level, however, perhaps their experience is tantamount to corruption. They cannot see how this story has corrupted them, but we readers can see it clearly. The double perspective was set up from the start of the poem, with the parallel opening lines of the first quatrain. It's also encoded into the metrical pattern of the poem. Starting off with a line of trochaic [a stress/ unstress pattern] in a tetrameter, the poem's lines alternate between the trochaic pattern and an iambic [unstress/ stress] one [The stressed syllables are in bold:

'I was **angry with** my **friend**
I **told** my **wrath** - my **wrath** did **end**
I was **angry with** my **foe**
I **told** it **not** - my **wrath** did **grow'**

How we read the poem, it seems, is a matter of our perception and how innocent, experienced, foolish or wise we are. What Blake calls 'single' vision is always limited and misleading in his poetry. Those blessed with double vision see more into the truth of things. But they're still just novices at the perception game. In Blake's poetry those with the most penetrating perception, perception that can open the gates of infinity to reveal the hidden secrets of the universe, have what he calls *four*-fold vision. They are the true visionaries.

A Poison Tree chopped down:

ANGRY - WRATH - FOE - GROW - WATERED - TEARS - SUNNED - DECEITFUL - GREW - APPLE - SHINE - MINE - GARDEN - NIGHT - GLAD - OUTSTRETCHED

Mary Lamb, *Envy*

Why is Mary Lamb's poem *Envy* in an anthology about conflict? Despite the sledgehammer effect of its title, which is wielded like an object destined to create blunt instrument trauma, it's a sweetly simple and straightforward poem. The title does give it away for sure, but envy does not necessarily create conflict. In fact, most envy, unless located in the plot of a soap opera or moral fable, is quite a private thing. And the conflict here is exactly that: an internal one, located deep in the self. More specifically, the conflict here is between what we are and what we aspire to be.

A metaphor by any other name...

Lamb has a simple yet highly effective extended metaphor, technically called a conceit, through which she conveys her message. The rose, itself almost a poetic cliché, is used in an unexpected way here. Rather than the rose symbolising an ideal love or beauty whose purity is beyond doubt here is means something much more complicated. The 'rose-tree' becomes tainted by envy and instead becomes impure as opposed to pure; it becomes 'a blind and senseless tree', determined 'to change its natural bent'. The imaginative corruption of this poetic symbol of pure love/beauty maximises the senselessness of irrational envy because it emanates from such a beautiful thing. Essentially, its 'pretty flower' and 'rose's scent' are irrelevant if the rose-tree cannot acknowledge or value these things; envy makes beauty ugly in Lamb's poem.

The extended metaphor of the rose-tree dominates the first two sestets before its human equivalent is given focus in the final stanza. Predominantly Lamb uses visual imagery to bring this envy soured rose-tree to life. Personification amplifies the strength of the envious emotions as it enviously eyes the alternative beauties of the 'violet blue' and 'lily fair'. The rose-tree's 'blind' spot is its inability to see and appreciate its own natural beauty. Instead it torturously envies the 'sweet mignonette' and ignores or has become oblivious to its 'own...rose's scent', a development that sees Lamb add an olfactory layer to her sensory imagery. Repetition of 'fret' and 'discontent' reinforces the emotional by-products of envy. While neither are particularly intense emotions their repetition shows how small niggling envies, if allowed to fester and multiply, can bring significant bitterness and even self-loathing into a person's life.

Repetition also builds sonic links between the first and second stanzas, creating a binding effect as if the envy is inescapable and confining; the fact that 'discontent' is one of the end-rhyme words increases the power of this repetition by making it boom out, amplifying the discontent envy brings. The strategy of repetition binding the stanzas together continues when Lamb repeats 'pretty flower' in the final line of the second stanza and the penultimate line of the final stanza. However, this repetition feels different as the 'pretty flower' changes from a confining, physical beauty to a limitless, internal beauty. The former suggests a downplaying of the rose's legendary beauty whereas the latter intensifies the beauty of wisdom and self-acceptance. This dual nature is reinforced by the sonics of the words themselves where the sharp, snappy plosive P and Ts exist in tension with the much softer L and R sounds; even the transition from narrow vowels [E and Y] to the long, broad O of 'flower' mimics a calmer, self-acceptance.

Accept yourself

This subtle sonic strategy is also seen in how the only alliteration in the entire poem makes the phrase 'care and culture' really stand out for the reader's ears. It's hardly surprising as these are the antidotes to envy, according to Lamb, and it suggests that 'care' both comes from within the self but also without, from 'culture'. Again, this makes perfect sense; envy is private, an individual obsession and Lamb argues that this must be dismantled in an idealistic pincer movement that is both individual and collective. While 'care' suggests individuals being nicer to themselves 'culture' could well mean 'society', suggesting that investing in wider social relationships is healthier than spending time festering alone in envy. 'Culture' could also feasibly be a synonym for 'art' and art therefore becomes a vehicle for self-discovery and imaginative self-regulation. Art and the craft of poetry is surely 'some talent that is rare' and while it could be described as a little-self-serving that the poet advertises her poem and the wider vocation of art as a key weapon in fending off envy's barbed attentions, it is undeniably relevant. No doubt this has to do with the ability of art to drag the reader/viewer out of one's self and into the type of empathetic imaginative scenarios that provide perspective.

Regardless, notice how the 'pretty flower' is superseded by 'talent that is rare', a process that moves the emphasis from inconsequential physical prettiness to a more wholesome solution. Lamb proposes that it's what you can do, not what you look like that will banish envy and nourish self-love. There's a sense of conflict here; the classic Platonic tension between the body and the soul. Envy, according to Lamb, is obsessed with the body, the mortal, the transient and that to avoid this requires a switching of attention to its binary opposite: the soul, the immortal, the transcendent. The fact that the antidote to envy is 'some talent that is rare' stresses the necessity of embracing our uniqueness and difference.

Some pretty flower of the mind

To reinforce the sweet, simple message of her poem Lamb employs a suitably simple, maybe even sweet, form. It is a very regular form with its identical stanzas and its relentlessly masculine rhymes.  The three sestets generate a soothing regularity that suggests the strength of self-confidence coming from within. However, all is not as simple as it seems. The sestets are internally divided into two triplets where the final line of each triplet drops two syllables as it moves from an iambic tetrameter to an iambic trimeter. For example:

> With **care** and **cul** ture **all** may **find**
> Some **prett** y **flower** in **their** own **mind**
> Some **tal** ent **that** is **rare**

The indented third line visually signals a change and the dropping of the two syllables reflects the type of simplification that is required to banish 'fret' and 'discontent'.

However, each sestet sees a cycle of simplification and complication that tells us that banishing envy is not easy; it's an ongoing process that requires rigorous self-discipline. Additionally, the very final end rhyme of 'rare' is not a perfect rhyme for 'are' - the only occurrence of such a weak rhyme in the poem. The poem does not end in confident sonic triumph, but instead in sonic uncertainty, perhaps implying that maybe it's not just the talent that is rare but the ability to live a life completely devoid of envy that is rare. This sonic weakness also suggests how even the most iron-willed of us is prone to envy.

The unusual rhyme scheme of AABCCB also reinforces the difficulty of

43

eradicating envy. There is a clear sonic separation balanced with a sonic togetherness, reflecting the isolation of individuals who see others together and who apparently have everything, whether that be platonic friendship or sexual companionship. Again, there's a tension between the sonic alienation of the rhyme scheme and the simplification of the trimeter end line that seems characteristic of the poem as a whole; banishing envy or even managing it seems to be an ongoing conflict between logical wisdom and irrational emotions. In the current culture of selfies and highly edited virtual lives projected through social media it seems a pertinent, artistically accomplished little poem for our times.

Crunchy
ROSE-TREE – LILY – SWEET – DISCONTENT – NATURAL – VAIN – FRET – OWN – GENTLE – SCENT – DISCONTENT – PRETTY – BLIND – IMAGINED – ENVIOUS – CARE – MIND – RARE

NB
Research the extraordinary life of Mary Lamb and it might seem surprising that such a tumultuous mind could produce such a seemingly wise and tranquil poem. There's world of difference, however, in expressing an idea beautifully and being able to live by it.

William Wordsworth, *Extract from The Prelude*

Conflict on the mind

On first reading, we might question the inclusion of the extract from *The Prelude* in a cluster of poems with the heading 'conflict'. The excerpt describes a young boy rowing a boat out into the middle of a lake and then returning; the potential for conflict seems limited. In *The Prelude*, nature does not actually change or do anything. However, what does change is the speaker's perception of nature, which leads to a disturbing transfer of power from the boy in the first half of the poem onto the natural world in the second half. Rather than a conflict that takes place externally in the outside world between people, the conflict of *The Prelude* extract is an internal one that takes place within the mind and emotions of the individual speaker.

Before we take a closer look at how the poem works, it is useful to reflect on the poem's context, form and structure. Wordsworth was one of the leading poets of the Romantic movement of the nineteenth century, an artistic and philosophical movement that sought to explore and explain the individual and his/her relationship to society and the natural world though the power of emotions and the imagination, rather than through rational and scientific enquiry. In particular, the Romantics saw the imagination and its interplay with nature as the key to attaining a deeper understanding of who we are and what the universe is really like, an insight which is central to understanding this extract from *The Prelude*.

When considering the poem's form and structure, it is also important to note that this extract is part of a much longer poem, *The Prelude or, Growth of a Poet's Mind*, which Wordsworth worked on for most of his adult life and which ran to almost eight thousand lines! Wordsworth had set out to write an epic poem to rival John Milton's monumental masterpiece, *Paradise Lost*. Epic poems are long narrative poems that explore historical or mythological events important to the culture in which they are written. Milton's poem traced the fall of Adam and Eve from the Garden of Eden into a world of sin and death; Wordsworth, in a turn of Romantic individualism, cast himself as the hero of his own epic and wrote *The Prelude* to examine the significant moments from his own life that had led him to becoming a poet and which had shaped his understanding of the world. However, like Milton, Wordsworth chose to compose his poem in blank verse, unrhymed lines of five stressed syllables usually with an iambic metre. This not only enabled Wordsworth to replicate the natural rhythms of everyday speech - a particular concern of the Romantic poets - but also gave him the flexibility to relate and unfold events for the reader in the naturalistic and organic way he actually experienced them, rather than distort experience by forcing it to conform to a strict rhyme scheme or inflexible metrical pattern.

One summer evening

The extract starts simply enough, with the young Wordsworth finding a small rowing boat moored by the side of a lake. The poet reveals that it was nature personified as a goddess or maternal force that led him to the boat, yet the parenthesis suggests this is the retrospective understanding of the older poet rather than an awareness of divine intervention - a characteristic trait of epic poetry - intuited by the young boy. In the second sentence, it is now the boat which is personified and feminised as the poet recalls how 'Straight I unloosed her chain, and stepping in/ Pushed from the shore'. The boy imagines himself almost as a heroic knight of Chivalric romance, liberating the helpless maiden in distress. There is no hesitancy in his actions; both lines start with a reversed metrical foot whereby the iambic pattern is substituted for a trochaic one so that the first syllables of each line 'Straight' and 'Pushed' are stressed. This creates a sense of urgency, confidence, forcefulness and determination to his actions. Urgency is further emphasised by the enjambment of 'and stepping in/ Pushed', which leaves little time to question the moral implications of taking the boat without permission. If the boy did pause to consider what the older poet recognizes as 'an act of stealth/ And troubled pleasure', it is quickly passed over as he rows the boat out onto the lake and witnesses 'on either side/ Small circles glittering idly in the moon /Until they melted all into one track/ Of sparkling light'. The scene is one of spectacular beauty where the ripples from the boy's oars reflect the moon's light and form a trail behind the boat where the heavens and the Earth seem to merge and become indistinguishable. Wordsworth's use of the present participles 'glittering' and 'sparkling' accentuates the immediacy of the experience and seem to bathe him in a celestial light, while the sense of being caught breathless by this moment of transcendent, heavenly vision is reproduced by his use of an expansive  sentence that spans seven lines. The way in which the ripples from the oars melt 'into one track' is also suggestive of the workings of memory, where seemingly random and inexplicable moments from our present recede into the past to be given retrospectively a shape and purpose that provide meaning and direction to our lives - a fitting emblem of Wordsworth's purposes throughout *The Prelude*. It is perhaps not by chance that the word 'I' echoes through these lines in the assonance of 'side', 'idly' and 'light'.

As the boy continues to row out into the lake, his confidence - possibly even arrogance - in his own skill and strength is once again made evident. The poet notes how he is 'Proud of his skill' as he dips his oars 'lustily' into the waters. The adverb here suggests the delight he takes in his own power and energy which verges on sexual excitement. The present participle 'heaving' further reinforces the sense of vigour and force, while the simile 'like a swan' reflects the boy's skilful and graceful mastery over the boat and the natural world  embodied by the lake. Epic poetry typically depicts the heroic exploits of mythological warriors and the metaphorical transformation of the small rowing boat into 'an elfin pinnace' suggests the younger Wordsworth was casting himself in such a role, a 'pinnace' being a small boat with several sails that was part of a warship, with the adjective 'elfin' helping to create the atmosphere of mystical enchantment. However, it is in the boy's 'unswerving line' as he fixes his eyes upon 'The horizon's utmost boundary' where the sense of complete dominance over his environment is most apparent. It is as if through the imagination and sheer will-power the boy intends his heroic quest to take him through the boundaries of the known universe. Wordsworth seems to enact this shattering of limitations by extending this line to twelve syllables rather than the expected ten. However, the disruption this causes creates a jarring effect, hinting that the boy's sense of control over the natural world is not as comprehensive as he currently believes. It is his mistaken belief that 'far above/ Was nothing but the stars and the grey sky', the assumption that he comprehends everything within his environs, which leads to the shock and disempowerment that Wordsworth relates in the second half of the extract.

A huge peak, black and huge

The whole extract turns on the word 'when', which appears roughly in the middle of the remarkable sentence that begins 'She was...' in line seventeen and ends with 'Upreared its head' in line twenty-four. This sentence has already guided the reader through four lines of the boy's triumphant journey into the centre of the lake, but as the speaker moves out of the shadow of the 'craggy ridge' (it is important to understand that as he been rows the boat forwards into the lake he is actually facing back towards the shoreline) a higher peak behind the first now suddenly becomes visible. Wordsworth delays the all-important verb 'upreared' until the very end of this extremely lengthy sentence to build tension and suspense, but also to evoke the boy's own confusion and bewilderment as the mountain rises ominously into view. The force of the shock lies in the boy's false and overconfident assumption that the first 'ridge' was the boundary of the horizon, so that there could be nothing else behind it. Whether he recognizes in the rational part of his mind that this emerging shape is a mountain is irrelevant; what matters is that in his imagination this shape is transformed into an indefinable and overwhelming creature or sentient force that now strides after him like the giant in a fairy tale chasing down the young thief. However, there is no heroic response in this tale. Instead, the boy's sheer terror is captured in the frantic repetition of 'I struck and struck again' as he attempts to outrun the nightmarish entity. Yet the further away he rows, the larger and more overpowering the mountain becomes, giving the appearance that the 'grim shape' is pursuing him as if an avenging, supernatural creature out of Gothic fiction.

But what most terrifies the boy is the mountain's sheer otherness; whereas earlier in the extract Wordsworth had personified and feminized both nature and the boat, it is significant that here the mountain is described twice with the pronoun 'it'. He cannot subdue or familiarize it through the power of his imagination and the failure of language is registered in the repetition of 'a huge peak, black and huge', where the plain, uninspired and repetitive diction contrasts  tellingly with the transcendent, highly poetic imagery deployed earlier in the poem. The boy is overwhelmed and his earlier confidence of mastery over the natural world is instantly destroyed. Instead, it is the mountain peak, and by extension, nature itself, which is filled with 'voluntary power' independent of mankind and infinitely more potent. What the boy discovers is that nature is not only beautiful but can also be sublime, evoking awe and terror at its uncontrollable power. It is this terror which is externalized onto the 'trembling oars' that propel the speaker back to the safety of the shore.

The final lines of the poem reflect on the significance of this life-changing experience. One thing the experience seems to have taught the boy is an awareness of moral culpability and guilt in the act of stealing the boat; the description of how he 'stole my way/ Back to the covert of the willow tree' draws attention to the act of theft not only through the verb 'stole', but also 'covert', which as a noun is another word for the 'cove' where he initially found the boat, but as an adjective carries the additional meaning of something done secretly. Repeated reference here to the 'willow tree' also highlights the associations of the tree with grief and sorrow, which implies an acceptance of guilt. On this reading, nature has acted like a stern parent, disciplining and correcting its child out of love, although this is something only understood by the poet as he reflects on what happened. This draws a parallel with Milton's rendering of Adam and Eve's story in *Paradise Lost* - the epic poem Wordsworth was consciously seeking to emulate - which also deals with the themes of pride, guilt, and divine correction.

Blank desertion

Yet there does seem to be more to this experience than just an acknowledgement of personal guilt. When Wordsworth notes how he returned home in 'grave/ And serious mood', we cannot help but hear the secondary meaning of 'grave' as a place of burial. It is possible the shock of encountering this unexplainable presence awoke in the poet an understanding of his own vulnerability, insignificance and mortality in the face of the great forces of nature which will long outlast any assertions of human power. But what seems most troubling for Wordsworth is the sense of an existential crisis that the experience triggers, whereby the poet's understanding and ability to give meaning to the universe is suddenly shattered. The adjectives 'dim', 'undetermined' and 'unknown' all point to his inability to fit the experience into any of his preconceived notions and categories. When he writes 'call it solitude/ Or blank desertion' he is really admitting he has no words to describe what he felt and can only settle for vague approximations. Instead, he can only define the experience by what it was not, as is accentuated by the triple anaphoric phrases, 'No familiar shapes', 'no pleasant images' and 'no colours of green fields', which echoes Milton once again through reference to a paradise that is now lost. The images of natural beauty have been supplanted by the 'huge and mighty forms' that represent the incomprehensible and untameable power of nature that oppress and overwhelm the young Wordsworth. The extract ends with disillusionment and disempowerment as the boy discovers he is not the master of his own world. Yet in removing this youthful delusion the way is now cleared for a more measured and sober understanding of the world and the poet's place within it, something Wordsworth continues to work out over the course the entire poem of which this extract forms just one small but significant part.

The Prelude crunched:

SUMMER – BOAT – COVE – UNLOOSED – STEALTH TROUBLED – MOUNTAIN-ECHOES – HER – MOON – MELTED – SPARKLING – PROUD – FIXED – SUMMIT – BOUNDARY – STARS – LUSTILY – DIPPED – BOAT – SWAN – BEHIND – HUGE – POWER – STRUCK – GRIM – TOWERED – PURPOSE – THING – TREMBLING – STOLE – COVERT – LEFT – HOMEWARD – MOOD – MANY – DIM – UNKNOWN – DARKNESS – DESERTION – NO – NO – MIGHTY – MIND – DREAMS.

Lord Byron, *The Destruction of Sennacherib*

Mad, bad and dangerous to know

Lord Byron [otherwise known as the satisfyingly alliterative '6th Baron Byron'] is variously described as 'flamboyant', 'notorious', and 'excessive'. He died in 1824 at the tender age of 36, after contracting a fever - perhaps from his flamboyant and excessive activities - and he is celebrated now as one of the leading figures of the Romantic movement.

The Destruction of Sennacherib retells the story of how the Assyrian army fell in 701 BCE/BC, documented in the Bible (2 Kings, Chapter 19). In reality, the city of Jerusalem actually paid tribute to Sennacherib after the event, but this detail is mysteriously missing from Byron's account, which is much more interested in the supernatural and all-powerful elements of how the Assyrians died. This is a well-known poem - so well-known, in fact, that, after defeating the English team, the victorious Australian cricket team of 1878 parodied it. Byron's poem describes the downfall of the Assyrian army at the hand of God.

A force powered by God

Byron was a major player in the Romantic movement in literature, which took as one of its main images the topic of nature. You can see this all the way through the poem, examples being 'like stars on the sea', 'leaves of the forest', 'blue wave rolls nightly' and 'sunset'. The Assyrians themselves are likened to the leaves falling and withering. This comparison is really important for two reasons:

1. Nature is based on eternal cycles. Examples of these are the seasons, the water cycle, and life and death. The second belongs to your Geography lessons, but the first and last are both central to this poem in which the seasons pass from 'Summer' to 'Autumn'. This is relevant because the deaths of the Assyrians are compared to nature: 'Like the leaves of the forest when Summer is green... Like the leaves of the forest when Autumn hath blown'. Just as nature will always push on with its inevitable and unchanging cycles, Byron shows us here that the triumph of God and the 'Angel of Death' over Sennacherib is also inevitable, unstoppable and fated to happen. It's just a fact of nature, part of the natural order. An order on which the Christian God is definitely at the top.

2. For the Romantics, nature was part of God's design, and it trumps everything else on earth. Nature was seen as all-powerful, a force stronger than humans, a force powered by God. In *Frost at Midnight* another Romantic poet, Samuel Taylor Coleridge, called nature an 'eternal language, which thy God / utters'. Nature, for these poets, is an eternally good, pure and omnipotent force. By saying that the destruction of the Assyrians is a part of nature, Byron is implying perhaps that their death was both a work of God and also a good thing. The 'Angel of Death' is a character who commands our awe and wonder - all it takes is for him to breathe 'in the face of the foe as he passed'. We are encouraged to think that the death of the Assyrians is justifiable and mighty.

What other examples can you find in the poem where nature is controlled by God? Why do you think this might be important?

Hungry like a wolf

How does Byron build up our opposition to the Assyrians? Firstly, the opening line tells us that 'The Assyrian came down like a wolf on the fold'. The image of the ravening wolf attacking sheep is a common one running throughout the

Bible and is used to represent the Devil attacking the vulnerable and good-hearted. This simile encourages the reader to feel that the predatory Assyrians are on the side of evil. Secondly, Byron says that the Assyrians are 'gleaming in purple and gold'. These are the colours of royalty, but specifically only really the colours of *modern* royalty; they wouldn't have carried the same symbolic significance in 701 BC. Probably, historically, the detail is very inaccurate. However, Byron is writing for an audience that knows what these colours mean to them; wearing purple was illegal in England from the Middle Ages until the 17th century, where it was restricted to royalty under the Sumptuary Laws. Whether you're one of Byron's friends reading this poem or reading it in the classroom in 2017, you can tell that Byron is talking about people who probably need taking down a peg or two. The 'sheen of their spears' is also all very artificial. If they were noble and experienced warriors, their weapons would have shown a little more wear and tear.

The Angel of Death

However, Byron also paints a sympathetic picture of the Assyrians' deaths. Byron says that 'the Angel of Death' only must pass over the army and their horses for their eyes to '[wax] deadly and chill'. Death is depicted as merciful, without pain or suffering [bear in mind that a total of 185,000 people died in real life at the Assyrian camp]. The action doesn't really obey the normal laws of time; instead, miraculously, the soldiers change state from living to dead seamlessly, 'and for ever grew still'.

Byron also uses an old-fashioned Biblical lexicon [the particular vocabulary of a person or branch of knowledge] such as 'strown', 'hath' and 'idols'. The Biblical diction gives the impression that this story is directly taken from the Bible, and therefore has the backing of both history and God. Lastly, the actions of The Angel of Death are supported in Byron's final stanza, where 'the idols are broke in the temple of Baal'. This battle happened *before* Christ was born, but likely *after* the Ten Commandments [dated between the 14th and 1st centuries BC] were written. The Commandments

command that keeping or observing idols [i.e. things or images that aren't God but are worshipped as gods] are most definitely, definitely not allowed.

The smashing of the idols in the Temple of Baal is another Old Testament story taking place around 150 years *earlier* in the 9th century BC; Byron is playing it really fast and loose with his squishing together of different Bible stories. However, it is the overall effect that's important - using the story of vanquishing false worshipping of idols to support the Destruction of Sennacherib. Imagine how different this story would be told from the Assyrians' viewpoint.

Galloping into oblivion

The poem is written in a fancy-sounding metre, the anapaestic tetrameter. That's a lot less complicated than it sounds. This is how anapaestic tetrameter goes:

dum dum **DUM** dum dum **DUM** dum dum **DUM** dum dum **DUM**

You can see this straight away from the opening lines:

'The AsSYRian came **DOWN** like a **WOLF** on the **FOLD**,

And his **CO**horts were **GLEAM**ing in **PUR**ple and **GOLD**'

The central quality of this rhythm is its swift, driving, upbeat force. This gives the poem tremendous energy and drama, and whilst the metre can be used for comedy - in a sing-song way - here it's utilised to make the subject matter vividly exciting and glorious. The three-beat unit [the anapaest] also echoes the three-beat rhythm of a horse's gallop - this is particularly war-like as they used cavalry so heavily at the time. Byron even focuses in on the war-horse as a victim of the 'Angel of Death'; 'And there lay the steed with his nostril all wide'.

The rhythmic drive of the poem is enhanced by the choice of the couplet form. Rhymes come thick and fast and each second line in a pair echoes the first and completes a rhythmic pattern that is then repeated consistently throughout the entire poem. Full, masculine rhymes add to the stressy, emphatic and dynamic quality of the verse. There's great assurance in the handling of the verse form and its demanding galloping metre; the poem hits and maintains its stride without any stumbles or hesitations. This technical dexterity reinforces the confidence with which Byron tells us this destruction is the work of God.

The Destruction of Sennacherib crunched:

ASSYRIAN – WOLF – PURPLE – LEAVES – FOREST – ANGEL – DEATH – BREATHED – DEADLY – CHILL – GASPING – COLD – DISTORTED – PALE – ALONE – WAIL – UNSMOTE – LORD

Emily Dickinson, *A Certain Slant Of Light*

Emily Dickinson is not a poet who explores the lighter side of life too often. She is a famously dark, philosophical poet whose abstract meditations can be quite off-putting for the uninitiated. To make matter more complicated she describes her poetic project as to 'Tell all the Truth but tell it slant'. Next Stop: Confusionsville! She is certainly gifted at approaching familiar topics from quite unusual angles/slants. On top of this is her unique metaphorical approach to subjects – 'Hope is the Thing with Feathers'; 'My Life had stood a Loaded Gun' – which makes her poems challenging poetic puzzles for professors the world over. Yet it is this very difficulty that makes her such a pleasure to study. Embrace her strangeness and the results will be many and rewarding.

Heavenly hurt

This brings us nicely to how Dickinson feels when viewing some lovely sunlight on a winter's day. What could be more uplifting? While we probably would expect such a burst of sun in dark winter to bring relief and enjoyment it has an unexpected effect on Dickinson's poetic speaker. Rather than bringing literal and metaphorical brightness it has the opposite effect, it 'oppresses, like the Heft / Of Cathedral Tunes'. Dickinson's Calvinist heritage, which sees her utilising the church hymn form for most of her poetry, would lead us to expect 'Cathedral Tunes' as a form of existential relief and soothing. However, the nouns 'Heft' and 'Tunes' combine to deliver an odd feeling of both oppressive overbearing and whimsical triviality. The onomatopoeic 'Heft' suggests

something big and ponderous, conveying Religion's clumsy and heavy-handed approach to dealing with the speaker's anguish. In contrast, the childish nature of 'Tunes' belittles religion's ability to offer any spiritual comfort. Whilst 'Tunes' could refer to cathedral bells, it could just as easily refer to church hymns, which would further trivialise their serious function. Predominantly Dickinson's poetry uses the ABCB rhyme scheme of the church hymn, but her rhymes mostly combine weak and strong sounds. Here the poem's rhyme scheme is relentlessly strong, with each rhyming pair booming confidently out of the poem, which seems at odds with the atmosphere of spiritual uncertainty and anguish the poem explores. It also, in a way, mimics the resounding 'Heft' of the 'Cathedral Tunes' that seem to aggravate rather than sooth the speaker.

An invisible invasion

This denigration of religion is continued when the speaker describes the 'certain Slant of Light' as causing 'Heavenly Hurt', with the alliteration of the H sounds connecting them to the 'Heft' of the previous stanza. A memorable oxymoron, akin to divine despair, 'Heavenly hurt' suggests exquisite pain, pain almost perfect in its ability to 'oppress' the sufferer. It also implies that heaven may have been hurt in some way, or rather, that this experience has hurt the poet's belief in or understanding of the Christian idea of heaven. Dickinson emphasises the invisibility and psychological nature of this trauma as it leaves 'no [external] scar' but rather creates 'internal difference / Where the Meanings are'. This is no passing blue mood but rather a seismic, soul-shattering, self-division that complicates the speaker's previous assumptions about profound 'Meanings'. The 'internal difference' brought on by external conditions seems to create a type of self-conflict that is devastating to the speaker.

It would be easy to dismiss the speaker as a complete mentalist, to be fair! The poem's entire premise seems pretty innocent and harmless, yet it is the unpredictable, sudden transition from 'certain Slant of Light' to the 'Look of Death' that is most frightening. Certainly, the speaker seems crippled by depression of the darkest strain and the insistence that this random trauma is seemingly 'Sent us of the Air' is one of its most terrifying aspects. Dickinson ascribes a name to it when she proclaims it 'Despair'. This word basically means 'hopelessness', but Dickinson complicates it by describing it an 'An imperial affliction'. This phrase connotes both sickness ['affliction'] but also something more profound. Continuing the theme of oppression from the first stanza, 'Imperial' can be seen as shorn of its religious connotations and connecting to the wider external forces that shape our destinies; irresistible, all engulfing forces that sweep us before them. That said, one can also see

 religious connotations in this 'Despair' caused by the 'certain Slant of Light'. In biblical terms, 'Let there be Light' is shorthand for the awesome creative power of God and references

to light are often associated with bestowing of divine knowledge/grace/purity etc. In this instance then 'imperial affliction' describes divine knowledge/power/presence as intruding upon the natural world, transforming something that should bring relief into something that brings dread. This feeling of dread is reinforced by Dickinson's skilful sonic patterns in the third stanza.

'Tis the Seal Despair –
An imperial affliction
Sent us of the Air –

The hissing sibilance of the S-sounds [and the F-sounds], the strong plosive P and T-sounds and the grating fricative C-sound combine to create a harsh sonic environment that reflects the speaker's mental turmoil.

The land of the living dead

Dickinson careens from the external to the internal and back again by the poem's end. But this time the external seems very much animated by the internal world of the speaker. The impact of the 'Slant of Light' creates an atmosphere of suspenseful fear and trepidation in the speaker and Dickinson uses personification effectively to show this. Like vulnerable prey praying for a predator to pass 'the Landscape listens' until 'it goes'. Alliterative L-sounds here are soft and gentle suggesting the vulnerability in the face of this great indescribable oppressive presence. Sibilance and strong, harsh fricative sounds are again notable. This time the sibilance creates a hushed, whispering atmosphere punctured by the presence of the sharp C-sounds. Even the 'Shadows' [normally connoting dark moods and hidden dangers] 'hold their breath', which intensifies the atmosphere of gothic menace. Rather than frightening, the shadows here are frightened. Again, to return to biblical matters, Dickinson creates a light that is more a Slash of light than 'Slant' where this overbearing, brooding presence seems a manifestation of the vengeful God that dominates the Old Testament.

If the final stanza begins with Life, it most undeniably ends with 'Death'. This is the final resounding word in the poem and its lethal power is emphasised by its rhyming word 'breath'. Structurally, in the stanza breath gives way to death. However, in typical Dickinson fashion, the presence of Death is not straightforward. When the odd, paralysing presence of the 'Slant of light' evaporates Dickinson doesn't express relief or urgent reengagement with the world, but, instead, something 'like the Distance / On the look of Death'. What the hell is she talking about?! It's a puzzling phrase for sure, whose obscurity is increased by being a simile where the thing compared to 'the Distance / On the look of Death' is not clear. The poem's inability to concisely describe or justify the crippling emotions of despair it explores is continued to the very end, leaving the reader as uncertain and potentially lost as the poetic speaker.

What are we to make of this terrifically odd simile? Is the poet describing the numbness and denial ['Distance'] that comes with experiencing the death of a loved one, aka getting a 'look' at 'Death'? OR is she referring to the detached, unemotional 'Distance' on the face of some personified grim reaper type figure? An almost indescribable impersonal expression of indifference? If we lean towards this latter interpretation the 'certain Slant of Light' takes on increased levels of Gothic terror, where it can be seen as not the light of God but the searchlight  of Death itself, seeking its next victim. Really it is not clear, but the common aspect to both interpretations is an emotional coldness that ends the poem in overwhelming pessimism.

Clinically compressed

Hyphens. Why are there so many of these pesky things running around the poem? It is also really saying something when this is one of Dickinson's more restrained poems in terms of hyphen usage! Dickinson uses hyphens in idiosyncratic ways and they are even more unconventional and avant garde jazz in the handwritten versions of her poetry. In general, a hyphen functions to join phrases or sentences together or to signify something cut off in the middle of being said. In Dickinson's poetry, where her condensed style seems to compress maximum poetic power into minimum poetic expression, the hyphens add to the compression by suggesting things unsaid and covered over by the poem. In this poem, most of the hyphens are at the end of lines, merely acting to connect them. However, there is still the niggling feeling that each hyphen could have lead somewhere else, as if a silent balancing phrase has been compressed into this mysterious punctuation mark.

This sense of mystery is at its most heightened at the start of the third stanza where the speaker tries to describe [in vain, ultimately] what they are experiencing: 'None may teach it – Any – / 'Tis the seal Despair'. The hyphens in this case mimic someone desperately searching for a way to articulate their experience and the '– Any –' seems like the start of a phrase that is cut off prematurely. This feeling of something cut off is reinforced by the fact that it only has six syllables when it would normally have eight. Furthermore, it doesn't really make sense; surely we would say 'None may teach it – None –' or 'None may teach it – Nobody –'. The hyphens also create dramatic pauses and while this seems quite natural at the end of a poetic line, in the final stanza they create great suspense where the 'Shadows – hold their breath –' making us wait with the shadows. This increases the sense of uncertainty, which definitely feels appropriate to the puzzling end of the poem.

The compressing effect is also seen in the poem's metrical form. Famously, Dickinson's work is characterised by her pretty free and easy use of the church hymn with its ABCB rhyme scheme and 8-6-8-6 syllable lines. Notably, in this poem the quatrains comprise of 7-5-7-5 syllable lines. Big deal, I hear you cry! However, this minor modification serves to compress the sonic heaviness of the poem by shaving off an unstressed syllable, contributing to the overbearing atmosphere:

>That o **ppres** ses, **like** the **Heft**
>Of Ca **the** dral **Tunes**

The poetic lines are in iambic metre, but just have the initial unstressed syllable shorn. While the first two stanzas follow this 7-5-7-5 pattern, the third stanza has 6-5-8-5 syllable lines and the final stanza has 8-5-8-5 syllable lines. Again, this probably may not seem of much significance, but, firstly, it introduces an element of unpredictability previously missing and secondly the 8 syllable lines are not iambic [unstressed, stressed], they are trochaic [stressed, unstressed].

>**When** it **comes** the **Land** scape **List** ens
>**Sha** dows – **hold** their **breath** –

Such switching of metrical patterns sees Dickinson alternating longer lines that fall off in sonic power with shorter lines full of compressed sonic power and in a way this seems to mimic the conflict between the vulnerable individual speaker and the huge powerful external forces that seem so oppressive and paralysing.

The woman in white

Literary scholars are not certain about the precise biographical facts, but the consensus is that when she was in her twenties Dickinson fell in love, probably with an older, married preacher called Charles Wadsworth. Though she shared some precious time with Wadsworth, it seems her love was not requited. Soon after Wadsworth moved far away Dickinson became a recluse, hardly seeing any visitors and dressing always in a white dress. In her letters from around this time the poet also wrote that she 'had a terror' that may have precipitated some sort of breakdown. The relation between unrequited love and the 'terror' isn't clear. Some scholars argue that Dickinson consciously withdrew from the outside world because she felt alienated by its attitudes and behaviour. Whether her withdrawal from the world was an entirely rational decision, whether it was triggered by rejection in love or by some kind of existential terror, like that depicted in *A Certain Slant of Light*, or by a combination of these pressures, we do not know. We do know, however, that the poet faced some sort of terrible crisis and became a permanent recluse.

A Certain crunch:

SLANT – WINTER – OPPRESSES – CATHEDRAL – HURT – SCAR – INTERNAL – MEANINGS – NONE – DESPAIR – AFFLICTION – AIR – LISTENS – SHADOWS – DISTANCE – DEATH

Thomas Hardy, *The Man He Killed*

Less is more

'Grandiloquence' is a word sometimes associated with Victorian literature and Victorian poetry in particular. It means language that is extravagant, designed to impress, rather puffed up and pompous. A grandiloquent poem is one in which the diction and phrasing have been inflated as if by over-vigorous application of a bicycle pump and varnished by over-vigorous application of elbow grease. Propagandist poetry aiming to inspire men to join up for WWI also tended towards the grandiloquent. Take, for example, these lines from an early Isaac Rosenberg poem exhorting men to war: 'Flash, mailed seraphim /your burning spears /New days to outflame their dim/ Heroic years...' and compare this heightened idiom to his later war poems, such as *Dead Man's Dump*.

One of the most remarkable aspects of Hardy's poem *The Man He Killed* [1902] is the complete absence of such verbal padding and straining after magniloquence. In fact, lean, clean and stark, Hardy's style in this dramatic monologue, written in the voice of an ordinary soldier, is the polar opposite. Language doesn't get much plainer or more direct than lines such as 'Had he and I but met, or 'I shot at him as he at me'. Each word is a simple, common monosyllable and these are arranged in the simplest of syntax too. In the first example that small word 'but' is made to carry huge weight and significance: But for one twist of fate the two anonymous men might have been friends. With its balanced, mirroring structure the syntax in the second example economically and powerfully communicates the similarity of the two men. A poet once defined poetry as using the fewest words for the most powerful impact. By this standard, Hardy's simple, plain style manages to be as least as expressive as more grandiloquent poetry.

Clear enough

The narrator presents his account in simple, stark terms. Simplicity in vocabulary is matched by a swift metre that leaves little time to pause, consider or reflect. Each brief quatrain has three short lines of trimeter and a slightly longer penultimate line of tetrameter, with a simple cross rhyme scheme. Mostly the tone is brusque, business-like, matter-of-fact, sticking doggedly to what happened, 'and [I] killed him in his place'. Can't get much plainer than that. In the third stanza the narrator seems, however, to become

more troubled. He feels the need to explain again why he killed this man towards whom he felt no personal animosity. A hyphen at the end of the first line and the repetition of the explanatory word, 'because' convey a pause in the account, a moment of uncertainty. This uncertainty continues and increases with the abrupt and unexpected internal rhyme of 'so', followed by another pause, a caesura and the reiteration of the fact that the man was a 'foe', creating another awkward internal rhyme. Repetition of this word 'foe' also makes it sound rather archaic in this context, like some sort of outdated concept. The clumsy syntax adds to the stuttering movement on this stanza, 'Just so: my foe of course he was'. Another off-hand sounding phrase, 'that's clear enough', with 'just so' and 'of course', ring ironically and immediately afterwards, the speaker seems to have doubts about his own assertions, 'although'. What is clear is that the speaker's feelings are deeply conflicted.

Whereas the two previous and the two following stanzas end neatly with full stops, enjambment connects the unfinished thought in the last line in this middle stanza to the opening of the following one. Working against the overt sentiments and apparent certainty of the words, the four hyphens in this fourth stanza are a continuing indication of the underlying uncertainty and hesitation. Again, the speaker links himself to the dead enemy, assuming that he may have joined the army 'off-hand like' just as the speaker had done. He assumes too that the dead man also shared a need for employment, being 'out of work'. It's a typically frank acknowledgement that the speaker did not join the army out of any romantic, heroic or patriotic notions. He just needed the work, simple as that, there was 'no other reason why'.

The final stanza begins with two euphemistic adjectives. Calling war and the twist of fate that led this speaker to kill that man he had no personal animosity for 'quaint and curious' is horribly, bitterly inadequate. This could, perhaps, indicate the speaker's inability to really comprehend his brutal experience. Pushing this further we could suggest this language implies a kind of brutish insensitivity.

But, I think, Hardy's point is more that his unnamed, everyman narrator doesn't have the language to express his complex and ambivalent feelings. Relief at his own survival is mixed with pity for his victim. And more than pity a sense of real empathy. It would be easier on the speaker's conscience if he gave in to the temptation to think of his victim as some sort of monster, or himself as some sort of hero following a noble cause. The switch in the last stanza from labelling his victim as a clearly demarcated 'foe' to simply a 'fellow' underlines this profound internal conflict.

Thomas Hardy was, of course, a novelist as well as a poet. Among his most famous novels are *Tess of the D'Urbervilles*, *Far from the Madding Crowd* and *Jude the Obscure*. In *The Man He Killed*, Hardy's novelistic skills come to the fore. He creates a distinct character and a strong sense of voice. And this soldier is also clearly an ordinary, decent man with generous instincts. Ordinarily he'd share a drink with this other man, 'treat' him and even give him money if he needed it. He has done his duty in war, but remains emotionally disturbed by his killing of another ordinary human being, and he has some sense that the ordinary soldiers might have more in common with each other than they have with other people, such as their commanding officers perhaps. The outer form of the poem expresses the character's outward appearance - business-like, unsentimental, neat, regular, brisk. But, closer up, behind the orderly facade the novelist ensures we detect the signs of a troubled conscience.

The Man He Killed crunched:

BUT - INN - WE - NIPPERKIN - INFANTRY - FACE - SHOT - KILLED - DEAD - BECAUSE - FOE - ALTHOUGH - PERHAPS - JUST - WORK - REASON - QUAINT - FELLOW - TREAT - HELP

Wilfred Owen, *Anthem for Doomed Youth*

What would you say was the single most remarkable thing about Owen's WWI poem? His use of sonic devices to create the sound scape of battle, such as the 'the stuttering rifle's rapid rattle/ can patter out' which mimics the rat-a-tat-tat of machine gun fire? Or the extended metaphor of the absence of funeral rites for these dead soldiers? Or, perhaps, that immediately striking first simile, for 'these who die as cattle'. Alternatively, you might suggest Owen's use of the sonnet form for a poem about war, but also about love. All of these are remarkable features, but, in my opinion the most remarkable thing about the poem is something absent from it; partisanship or animosity towards the enemy, the Germans.

The Hun

To fully appreciate how remarkable this absence is we have to wind the clock back and think ourselves into a young man's mind. An average young man, inspired to take up arms to defend his country, defend Europe, in fact, from German aggression. A young man who had swallowed all the propaganda he had been fed about the Great War, how it was going to be a terrific adventure, how he was going to return a hero, how the war was going to be short and swift, how the enemy was some sort of ravening, brutish monster and had to be stopped. In particular the mother country and her women needed protecting from the German beast. Here's 'The Hun', depicted in American propaganda as a sort of giant ape, King Kong type monster making off with a semi-naked, helpless damsel. This image may be American, but  British ones were just as bad. Demonising your enemy, of course, is a common strategy in propaganda. Probably by the time the Great War had begun the average English Tommy had been brainwashed into thinking of the Germans soldiers as brutal monsters.

Inevitable corollaries to anti-German feeling at a time of war were nationalistic and jingoistic fervour about England and Englishness. Read, for example, Rupert Brooke's *The Soldier*, a celebratory hymn to England, to catch the flavour of these sentiments. Of course, as the title indicates patriotism is expressed in Anthem for Doomed Youth, except that the national boundaries of England and Germany have been replaced by a generational one, the 'doomed youth' of both nations. Owen's poem is as much a lament for young, dead German soldiers as it is for the young English dead. At a time of war, considering the context of virulent propaganda, this seems remarkable.

It's an odd sort of anthem. Think of national anthems for a moment. Imagine you are a committee choosing a new one for a new country. What are you looking for? What are the key attributes of a successful national anthem? That it should be uplifting, stir the soul, have a feel of grandeur and impressive scale, celebrate the unique identity of the country and its history. Think of *Land of Hope and Glory*. Owen's poem certainly isn't rousing. It's a dirge or a lament, a song for the dead. Owen's choice of the word 'anthem' is bitterly ironic.

What passing-bells

As we mentioned at the start of this essay, Owen's poem is constructed around an extended metaphor, technically known as a conceit, comparing the soldiers' deaths on the battlefield with the rituals of a funeral: Rather than having 'passing-bells' the men are led away to be brutally and casually slaughtered, like 'cattle'; instead of last prayers [orisons] for their eternal souls, they have the pounding of artillery and the rattle of rifle fire; instead of mourners and a choir they have wailing shells and bugles. The second stanza, the sonnet's sestet, instead of candles, the only 'holy glimmers' they will see are in each other's eyes before death comes; rather than a funeral pall over their coffin they will have only the pale faces of their loved ones left behind in England and in lieu of flowers these women's tenderness. Finally, instead of having the blinds drawn as a sign of mourning, these men will face a greater darkness, that of night falling. The implication is that not only are these men led to slaughter, but that their sacrifice is not even adequately acknowledged or mourned for, let alone honoured. Perhaps even their chance of an afterlife is being denied. By whom? By the army, perhaps, and also by a population back home who had little idea of the true horrors - the gas attacks, going over the top, the barbed wire, the dead and dying in no-man's-land, the rats, the lice, the endless mud, the dead bodies, the ceaseless pounding of the big guns, the closeness of death, the blasted landscapes - of prolonged trench warfare. Like his friend and fellow war poet, Siegfried Sassoon, Owen wanted to puncture the complacency of the civilian population and try to get over to them the realities, truth and pity of the Great War.

So, perhaps, rather than the Germans, the real enemies were the callousness of the Generals sending men to be butchered, the indifference of the civilian population and the politicians who continued the war. Certainly Sassoon thought so and he famously said so in a letter published in The Times newspaper. Sassoon would have faced the severest of military discipline if his friends had not managed to plead he was suffering from temporary insanity and ship him off to Craiglockhart hospital in Scotland where Sassoon would

71

meet Owen for the first time. But there's another enemy in this poem and it appears in many of Owen's WWI poems.

A machine war

Sometimes in Owen's poems it can appear that nature and perhaps even God have either abandoned or actively turned against the soldiers. But a more persistent threat is the technology of warfare. WWI was the first 'machine war'. Though machine guns had been used previously, in the Boer War for instance, the ones used in WWI were far more efficient and deadly. Added to this was the new horror of gas shells and towards the end of the war, tanks and fighter planes. In *Anthem for Doomed Youth* Owen uses personification in a bitterly ironic way. It seems that as the men are dying helplessly the

 machines are taking on a life and a will of their own. It is almost as if the weaponry is acting of its own accord,

following its own mad logic without any human influence. There is a monster here, but it's not the German army; Owen describes the sound of the big guns [English and German] as 'monstrous anger'. He also uses the adjective 'stuttering' to describe rifle fire. This word suggests the intermittency of the firing, but also implies that the rifles might jam. More importantly, it is as if the weapons are speaking - they 'patter out' the men's prayers. 'Patter out', of course, can mean 'make the sound of', but also implies cancelling out, erasing. The shells are also personified, as a choir of 'shrill, demented' voices, 'wailing'. The madness and anger and monstrosity of the war seem to emanate from the technology; the soldiers are helpless before it.

Noticeably the imagery in the first stanza is predominantly aural. We hear the discordant din of battle, the anger, the stuttering, the wailing, guns, rifles, shells, bugles. The imagery of the second stanza is more visual and the atmosphere is more elegiac. In particular, Owen uses the symbolism of light, specifically light going out in references to candles, eyes, glimmers, pallor and finally dusk falling.

Owen's poem has to stand it for the absent mourning and funeral rites for the dead soldiers. He offers his lament as a way of honouring these 'doomed youth'. They were doomed because they faced impossible, insurmountable odds. Yet Owen, who was invalided to Craiglockhart with shellshock, chose to go back and fight with his men. Owen had the choice to sit out the rest of the war, but, knowing the full horror of the experience he chose to go back. He was a captain in the British army and he could not bear the thought of abandoning his men. It was a decision, of course, that cost him his life at the tender  age of just 25. Not only in his poetry then, but with his life, Owen demonstrated his deep respect, compassion and sense of honour for his fellow soldiers.

Anthem for Doomed Youth crunched:

CATTLE – MONSTROUS – RATTLE – PATTER – PRAYERS – CHOIRS– DEMENTED – BUGLES – SPEED – EYES – GOOD-BYES – PALL – TENDERNESS – DUSK

Keith Douglas, *Vergissmeinnicht*

The tanks that broke the ranks

They say that the First World War was the first modern war. Certainly, it was the beginning of the end for traditional hand-to-hand combat, as rifles and bayonets and horses, the symbols of centuries of warfare, began to be replaced by long-range artillery, bomber planes, trenches, chemical attacks and tanks. But it was during the Second World War that the lethal potential and terrifying implications of the new species of impersonal and deathless mechanical weapons began to be fully recognised and exploited. This new ability to kill [or to be killed] remotely, without having to look the enemy in the eye and sense a shared humanity, meant that killing became yet more dispassionate, breeding a cynicism which built on the already-tarnished reputation of the 'glorious war'. The poets of the Second World War responded by producing a body of work which detailed their experiences in an impassive, unsentimental voice. And none was more unsentimental than Keith Douglas.

Douglas had completed his officer training at Sandhurst in February 1941 and, after a brief stint with the 2nd Derbyshire Yeomanry, had been transferred to the Sherwood Rangers, and posted first to Palestine and then to Egypt. Egypt was a key territory in the Western Desert campaign, and El Alamein, the site of a railway halt, was one of its most strategically important regions. It was there [as the name suggests] that the Second Battle of El Alamein took place: a brutal conflict with vicious encounters between opposing divisions of armoured vehicles, which cost the Axis around 50,000 men and 500 tanks in the three weeks of fighting, and the Allies some 14,000 and 400 of the same. On the third day of the battle, after disobeying an order to remain behind, Douglas had led his tank division

into the fray, and before long had been hit square by the shell of an anti-tank gun. It was a face-to-face encounter with death, and yet, remarkably, none of his crew was killed, and they managed to destroy the gun-pit before it could fire on them again.

Three weeks passed and the battle finished, and Douglas and his men returned 'over the nightmare ground' and 'found the place' where their tank had been hit. They found, too, the bloated and rotting corpse of the soldier who had attacked them unsuccessfully, and whom they had killed, sprawled in the shadow of his anti-tank gun. It was this experience that provided the narrative for **Vergissmeinnicht**, one of Douglas' most celebrated poems, and one in which he most powerfully evoked the desensitising effect of the new mechanical warfare.

Cleanin' my rifle [and dreamin' of you]

A key conceit for Douglas in capturing this cynicism and callousness is his blurring of the boundary between animate and inanimate, between flesh and blood and cold hard steel. As the soldiers are losing their humanity, Douglas

75

seems to suggest, their weapons are gaining it. In the second stanza, for example, he personifies the 'frowning' barrel of the dead man's gun, ascribing it a human face with the vaguely displeased expression of the cartoon Army General: an expression whose indifference fails to convey the full horror of the blood-soaked scene. Later, Douglas has the adjective 'gunpit' qualify the unusual noun 'spoil', which can mean valuable items which have been pillaged or stolen, or the arms and armour of a slain enemy, but can also mean the uneaten remains of an animal carcass. Part of the effect here is in demonstrating that the poet has grown insensitive to death and suffering, and feels little guilt in dehumanising the dead German, reducing him to meat for scavengers to pick at. But part of the effect, again, is in breathing life into the inanimate steel: 'spoil' can be read as referring to the remnants of the destroyed 'gunpit', with the poet reimagining the ruined weapon as a dead and mutilated body, the machinery once more ascribed the attributes of a living creature.

Douglas extends this conceit when he describes how the dead soldier's lethal 'equipment' is 'mocking' the man who once operated it, attributing to the weapon the capability of human-to-human interaction. And when those two lines are read in full – 'mocked at by his own equipment / that's hard and good when he's decayed' – a sexual euphemism playing on 'equipment' and 'hard' becomes unmistakable. The lines provide more evidence of the cold-heartedness which the war has engendered in the speaker, in this case by recording the crude-ish joke he's made about a guy he's killed. But the image of the still-living weapon, unhurt and un-decayed, laughing at the frailty of the human body, also projects a vision of a world in which the machines have outlived their operators. Sex is a symbol of life, vitality and the continuation of the species, and is one of the fundamental interactions between humans. The dead soldier's 'decayed equipment' – his sexual impotency – therefore, reflects the broader demise of common human interaction, the loss of sympathy and sensitivity, and reads as a forecast of extinction.

There is a definite sense that the inanimate weapons have taken control of the soldiers' actions; that the soldiers have become more a tool of the weapons than vice versa. After all, 'mockery' isn't a balanced human interaction: it establishes a hierarchy which, in this instance, places the dead man's 'own equipment' above him. This reversed-ranking was hinted at in the poem's second stanza, where Douglas describes the barrel of the German's gun 'overshadowing' him – 'overshadow' can of course mean 'to cast a shadow over', but its other meaning of 'to diminish the relative importance of' is equally relevant here. And the peculiar simile, 'like the entry of a demon', in that same stanza introduces a motif of demonic enchantment, as if the rise of mechanical weaponry has acted like a malicious spirit, possessing the soldiers and driving them to  cruelty. It's a motif which seems to be continued in the poem's final stanza where, in the line 'And Death who had the soldier singled', Douglas appears to portray himself as the Grim Reaper [he killed the man, after all]. No wonder, then, that those still living feel distant and callous: they've lost their compassion, and they've surrendered control to the pitiless demon of war.

Don't let's be beastly to the Germans

In another of his poems, *Desert Flowers*, Douglas acknowledged his debt to the First World War poet, Isaac Rosenberg: 'Rosenberg I only repeat what you were saying'. But the narrative of *Vergissmeinnicht* is more reminiscent of a work by another Great War poet, Wilfred Owens, titled *Strange Meeting*. In that poem a soldier enters the underworld and meets an enemy soldier he had killed the previous day, just as Douglas returned and saw the man his crew had killed. Douglas' poem, though, is far more cynical and far less conciliatory than Owens', with the mutual respect and pity which the soldiers of *Strange Meeting* exhibit replaced by cruelty and derision and little success in taking a non-partisan view of the slaughter.

The gloating tone of the 'equipment' pun is far from the only instance of the speaker's mercilessness. He plays on the idiom 'with contempt' in the line 'We see him almost with content', simultaneously conveying the disdain the men feel towards the German and their delight in seeing him dead. He contrasts their nonchalant response with that of the dead man's lover who 'would weep', reinforcing the lack of tears with the image of the dry 'dust' on the 'paper eye', and seeming to revel in his breezy description of the swarming flies and the erupted belly. And he casts scorn on the signed photograph which they find among the soldier's possessions, a gift from his girlfriend back home, with the bathos of 'who has put' initiating the sneering tone, and the childish connotations of 'copybook' writing reinforcing it.

The adjective 'gothic' seems pointedly chosen, too: though it is commonly used to refer to the blackletter typeface often associated with written German, the word can also mean 'barbaric' or 'savage' or, most pertinently, 'in bad taste'. These alternative connotations serve to convey the speaker's feeling that the woman's gift too soppy and sentimental, and the Hollywood overtones

 of the carefully-placed 'script', coupled with the fact that *Vergissmeinnicht*, as well as being an expression and the name of a flower, was the title of a saccharine German love song from that era, certainly suggests that he thinks little of the sugar-coated romanticism on display. Moreover, the speaker seems determined to destroy any vestige of genuine emotion which the signed photograph may carry, insisting that it has been 'dishonoured' – there's a chance he means that it has been sullied by its proximity to death, but it seems more likely, considering the gloating tone elsewhere, that he means the girl has been dishonoured because her boyfriend lost the battle and got himself killed.

There is almost no honour paid to the dead throughout the poem, culminating in the final stanza which, despite its celebrated delineation of the soldier's twin identities, 'the lover and killer', reads more like a parody of wartime oration than a heart-felt reflection on the complex cruelty of war. The self-consciously Latinate inversion of 'who had the soldier singled', placing the verb at the end, does some of the work; the knowing archaism of 'mortal hurt', borrowed perhaps from *Romeo and Juliet*, finishes the job. Indeed, there seems to be an attempt to deny the dead German any value at all: that curious pun, 'We see him almost with content', could also be read as 'We see him almost with meaning' or 'with substance', with the implication being, 'Almost, but not quite'. This is supported by a proliferation of words relating to things not being fully real or of full value: 'almost' and 'seeming' are self-explanatory; 'abased' can mean 'degraded' / 'humbled', and can be used as a synonym for when currency is debased; 'mocked' contains the root 'mock' which can mean 'imitation' or 'counterfeit'. The dead German is unreal, the girlfriend's suffering is unreal – it's hard to find meaning and value, it seems, in the middle of the War.

Down forget-me-not lane

And yet, in that line, 'We see him almost with content', there is the feeling that Douglas and his crew are trying to see the dead German as real and valuable, but are simply unable to do so. The foregrounded opposition between that line and 'But she would weep to see today' demonstrates that the speaker recognises that the matter is purely subjective, that his perception of the situation is bound to be biased. He is, perhaps, more enlightened than others in acknowledging that, really, the German's life was worth no less than his own, at least to some people. But he is not so advanced as to be able to shed his patriotism and ingrained hatred of the Hun. History is written by the winning side, as it is here, and the sense of history – or, more, the sense of regression – runs strongly through the poem.

There are the archaisms highlighted above, to which might be added 'combatants', 'dishonoured' [with its connotations of chivalry], 'gothic' [in the sense of 'Germanic'], 'spoil' and 'swart'. They are words of earlier confrontations, with the Goths, with the 'swarthy' fighters of the Ottoman Empire, in which honour could be won and lost, and the spoils of war were the ready reward. And now they have resurfaced, lost once but returned again, as the repetition of 'gone' and 'found' in the poem's first stanza implies. The weapons may be different, but the inability to avoid bloodshed which marks millennia human existence is just as powerful as ever. Douglas sees in the scene, and in his own reaction to  the sight of the dead German, a powerful hand dragging him back into the past, into the primitive 'cave' of the man's 'burst stomach', which recalls not only rudimentary human life, but Plato's allegory of enlightenment [and the lack of it]. The 'dust' on the dead man's eye isn't just the sand of the desert: it's a reminder of the repetition of history and the inevitability of death; the same dust as in T.S. Eliot's 'I will show you fear in a handful of dust'; the same dust as the Bible's 'you are dust, and to dust you shall return'.

Douglas is suffering from a painful contradiction: there are faint traces of sympathy for the dead man, most evident in 'nightmare', perhaps, or 'who had one body and one heart'; but he is unable to escape the machinations of the civilisation which would have him feel no pity for the enemy, and has found his powers of compassion blunted by the remoteness and lottery of mechanised warfare. The inconsistency of the rhyme scheme – which shifts between ABBA, ABAB and AABB – and the use of pararhymes, which clashes, for example, 'heart' and 'hurt', seem to be a poetic embodiment of this contradiction. The gesture towards a rhyme-pattern is an attempt to make coherence and lyricism from brutality; the 'failure' of the rhyme scheme is the triumph of savagery and cynicism.

Vergissmeinnicht crunched:

COMBATANTS – NIGHTMARE – AGAIN – SPRAWLING – FROWNING –
OVERSHADOWING – TANK – DEMON – SPOIL – DISHONOURED –
VERGISSMEINNICHT – COPYBOOK – GOTHIC – CONTENT – ABASED –
MOCKED – HARD – WEEP – SWART – DUST – CAVE – MINGLED –
BODY – DEATH – MORTAL

Denise Levertov, *What were they like?*

Born in England, Levertov was a poet who spent considerable time at one of the frontlines of war as a civilian nurse in London hospitals during the worst fighting of WWII. She had no formal education and at the age of 12 she sent off some poems to T. S. Eliot, who responded in depth to her writing, offering her 'excellent advice'. Aged 24 she moved to the U.S.A. is now considered a fundamentally American poet.

Here she is writing about the Vietnam War, which took place between the North and South factions of Vietnam between 1955 and 1975. America backed South Vietnam, along with other countries opposed to the communist Soviet Union. There are many examples of war crimes, such as the murder of unarmed civilians by American forces, and the use of Agent Orange - a chemical weapon designed to destroy forest cover for the North Vietnam troops - caused longstanding health problems for civilians and soldiers alike. The images and reportage of the Vietnam conflict, such as the Napalm Girl and the self-immolating monk, have had a huge impact on how we think about war today.

Construction

Throughout the Vietnam War reportage and coverage of daily suffering filled people's screens and newspapers. Journalism is always a form of storytelling in itself - people working for newspapers choose which details to include, which to exaggerate or emphasise, and which to ignore. This poem has storytelling woven through the text. The structure indicates that someone with some authority [he is addressed as 'sir'] is asking a series of numbered questions. We are not told who this questioner is; perhaps they are journalists. Or a member of the American public. Or even descendants of the people who died. In the second stanza their questions are answered in turn by another anonymous voice. Though this voice attempts to provide answers, it becomes clear that the history and culture of the Vietnamese people has been lost, obliterated by conflict.

Of course stories are vital components of culture, and in particular there are lots of folklore versions in all sorts of different cultures which tell us of how we came to be created. Cultures such as Classical Greece told of a cosmic egg that gave birth to all humankind. In Vietnam, the myth is that a giant spider, Âu Co', hatched the first hundred ancestors to the Vietnamese people. The tone of the first stanza could be read in many different ways; it certainly has an enquiring tone, full of questions about what 'the people of Viet Nam' did during the Vietnamese War, but these stories are about their destruction – not their creation. The first part of the poem has the air of children clustered around an old grandmother, asking for stories of a forgotten past.

Taking what is known as 'faux-naif' perspective, i.e. one that pretends to be ignorant, Levertov makes us imagine a future scenario in which the culture of Vietnam and its people have been almost entirely wiped from the face of the earth. These people and their culture can only be reconstructed, pieced back together from the remaining fragments, through memories and stories, both of which are uncertain and unreliable sources. The poet emphasises the unreliability through hedging words, such as 'perhaps' and 'maybe', and by the repeated use of the mechanical-sounding phrase 'it is not remembered'. A whole culture and a world is condensed into that tiny pronoun, 'it'. And the passive construction masks the custodians of memory - 'it' is not remembered by whom? By the winners who got to write the history books, perhaps? By those who choose not to remember their victims?

Further examples of uncertainty and potential unreliability are found in the 'peaceful clouds were reflected in the paddies'. The speaker isn't looking directly at the clouds, but at their reflection. This is significant because that image of peace and tranquillity is only a hazy reflection. The line closely following - 'maybe fathers told their sons old tales'- has lots of words that indicate distance and ambiguity. The tales are 'old' to begin with, and then  the fathers tell them, meaning that even the 'old tales' are second-hand. Even then, it's only that the fathers 'maybe' tell them. Levertov does this to show how hard it is to accurately report and pass down stories from person to person, from culture to culture. In lines 27-28, 'there is an echo yet / of their speech which was like a song'. This reflects the fact that the stories of suffering flip further and further away from us if we are not able to keep hold of them and report them accurately, passing them down from generation to generation like when 'fathers told their sons old tales'. Echoes distort and mimic sound, but are never able to replicate the original.

Through western eyes

Caught up in this reporting is a reductive description of the lost Vietnamese culture. A reductive description is one that simplifies a complex idea, often in a way that shortcuts and distorts the truth. The first speaker certainly has distinct ideas about Vietnamese culture, implying that it was gentle, innocent, quiet, happy, reverential to nature and artistic. Images such as 'lanterns', 'ivory', 'jade', 'ceremonies', 'silver' and the idea that Vietnamese people can't 'distinguish between speech and singing' form a very Western perspective, in particular because of our bias in thinking about Asia as oriental, spiced, gemstone-y and florally exotic. It's

interesting that Levertov throws an 'epic poem' into this mix - an epic poem normally comes from the Greek classical tradition [and is therefore a Western idea]. It's easy to ignore the fact too that her poem is in English, but this further highlights how Vietnamese is being understood through Western perceptions.

Written in 1967, Levertov's poem was part of a much wider protest movement that rose up to oppose the continuation of the Vietnam War. Among the protestors were students, academics, film stars, famous musicians and other writers. Like other work from this time, the poem conveys an anti-war, perhaps idealistic message, emphasising not only the shared humanity of the combatants, but presenting the Vietnamese people as innocent victims of unexplained and obliterating aggression. Levertov's political poems, especially ones concerning the Vietnam War have subsequently come in for

some strong criticism, however. Some critics accused her of being moralistic, preachy and sentimental. The picture generated of a peaceful Vietnamese culture in the first stanza might be an example of this sentimentality. It's certainly hard to believe such a culture would ever go to war. Against this charge, other critics have argued that there's a humanism and empathy underpinning her best work.

As a contributor to the ironically long-titled Concise Dictionary of American Literary Biography put it, 'the emphasis in her work is on uniting cultures and races through an awareness of their common spiritual heritage and their common responsibility to a shared planet.'

Destruction

A corollary to the description of Vietnamese culture, in this poem the images of nature also convey a gentleness and calmness that is almost dream-like and passive. 'Gardens' are described as being lined by 'pleasant ways', peasants' [lives were] in rice and bamboo', 'peaceful clouds were reflected in the paddies' and even the big, strong 'water buffalo stepped surely along terraces' of rice. In contrast, the images of man-made things are chilling, violent and destructive. The contrasts can be brutal; straight after a description of people 'gathered' to 'delight in blossom' comes the bluntly factual 'after their children were killed'. The shadow of napalm haunts the poem in references to burning, such as 'the burned mouth' and 'all the bones were charred'. The bucolic calm of the paddy fields is 'smashed' to smithereens by 'bombs'.

Levertov uses sibilance in lines 25-31 to gradually decrease the intensity of image from 'scream' to 'silent'. We are taken from 'smashed' through 'scream', 'speech', 'song', 'singing', 'say' and 'silent; this reflects the silencing process of death and the wiping out of a culture and its people. The visceral agony of 'scream' is replaced by numbed silence. 'Their singing resembled /the flight of moths in moonlight' is a beautiful, romantic image. It brilliantly transforms sound into something visual, song to moths, and the metaphor of moths is apposite. Moths are small, delicate and short-lived creatures, drawn to the light that kills them. Moth flight is uncertain, flickery and moonlight is soft, but inconstant. It is a metaphor that captures in one memorable image the poem's whole perception and perhaps misperception of Vietnamese culture.

Piecing the fragments

Take a pencil and put a bracket to the sides of lines to reflect how many lines a sentence is broken up. Peaceful, serene images of 'water buffalo' span three lines, as do peasants and their 'life... in rice and bamboo'. The shorter sentences are clustered in the middle of the poem, with 'A dream ago, perhaps. Ornament is for joy. /All the bones were charred. /It is not

86

remembered. Remember'. These short sentences issue a series of snapshot images, not quite whole and not really expanded upon - they are tense glimpses of the fragments, 'all the bones'. The bones of humans represent the human wastage in war through dehumanisation- the lack of any other details about these people or their lives makes the image much more macabre and horrific, and reduces the human experience to that of pain, death and dismemberment. In particular, Levertov shows us how people literally break down to physical parts through war; 'their light hearts turned to stone', 'laughter is bitter to the burned mouth', and the ethereal 'singing'.

What Were They Like? crunched:

VIETNAM – LANTERNS – REVERENCE – SPEECH – SINGING – STONE – DELIGHT – CHILDREN – KILLED – LAUGHTER – BITTER – BAMBOO – PEACEFUL – BOMBS – SMASHED – SCREAM – REPORTED – MOONLIGHT – SILENT

 Is Levertov's dialogue really a poem? Imagine you're a poetry traditionalist; what arguments might you put forward to substantiate the claim that this just isn't really a poem? It has no metre, no rhyme, no stanzas...Now switch positions and be Levertov. How might you justify your poem? If you're working with another pupil, perhaps, you could take sides and stage a short debate. Which side do you find more convincing?

Gillian Clarke, *Lament*

One of the most memorable things about Cormac McCarthy's famous post-apocalyptic novel *The Road* is that the cause of the apocalypse is never revealed. For a plausible answer please see Gillian Clarke's furiously sad *Lament*. Clarke's title points to the sad ruefulness that is just one emotional tone of her poem – it is a poem of mourning for a world about to die. The anaphora of the repeated 'For...' gives us a whole list of victims lost in the global tragedy. It's an interesting list of victims: mostly its sea-life, either birds ['cormorants, 'terns' and 'waders'] or mammals ['dolphins,' 'dugongs' and 'whales'] or cuddlier sort of reptiles ['turtles']. The unfairness of such a loss is obvious and the victimisation straightforwardly appalling. In times of anxiety about unregulated eco-change the poem explores familiar territory.

While the poem laments the inevitable destruction of these natural beings lamenting humans is much more complicated. The only human presence in the poem is that of the soldiers and they're not the noble, heroic sort. Instead Clarke laments their ordinariness, their naivety and powerlessness to be anything other than pawns in much greater political machinations. The personalisation of the situation, 'Ahmed at the closed border' immediately brings us to the Middle East and various gulf wars, which is also reinforced by the reference to a well-known photograph of a British soldier in flames: 'For the soldier in his uniform of fire'. Consonance of the fs give the line an appropriately unsettling sizzling noise. Not only do we have the odd juxtaposition of the individual 'Ahmed' with the faceless 'soldier', 'gunsmith' and 'armourer', Clarke juxtaposes soldiers in peril with soldiers whose peril is their own stupidity! War being fought by 'the boy fusilier who joined for the company' is only slightly less worrying that 'the farmer's sons, in it for the music'. The point here is that it is not war per se that is the problem but the rampant stupidity that drives war that is most problematic. Conflict then is not just restricted to humans; the ecological consequences elevate the poem into a much more profound meditation on the ongoing war between humankind and the natural environment that supports and tolerates us.

There will be blood!

While Paul Thomas Anderson's 2007 film *There Will Be Blood* only suggested the ecological trauma of oil drilling here Clarke brings it clearly and undeniably into the foreground. The poem stinks of politically motivated war and brings to mind immediately the two Gulf Wars of 1990 and 2003. Both Gulf Wars were led by the US and British governments and both  governments were suspected of having ulterior motives of controlling Middle Eastern oil supplies.

The continuous references to burning in the poem echo strongly the media images of oil wells burning in these conflicts. However, Clarke amplifies the burning from just mere oil wells into a much more apocalyptic blaze. The poem begins with oil smothering the natural world. The cormorant is oppressed by 'funeral silk', a highly effective visual image combining the blackness and slickness of the polluting oil. This oil creates a gigantic, ominous 'shadow on the sea'. However, as most right thinking humans know oil and fire are a dangerous combination and it is no surprise that as the poem progresses 'the

missile's thunder' leads to a global conflagration resulting in the visceral images of a 'burnt earth' and a 'scalded ocean'. The poem's last sentiments are ones of jaded hopelessness, as if the poem itself has been reduced to 'the ashes of language'. This is undoubtedly the language of Christian apocalypse.

Furthermore, there are strong religious connotations to the 'ocean's ... mortal stain' and the 'shadow [of death] on the sea'. In the Christian tradition such phrases have connotations of death and murderous wrongdoing, i.e. the mark of Cain. But in the poem it is very much man's ecological sin against the beautiful fertility of nature that is condemned. 'The green turtle with her pulsing burden' symbolises nature's fecundity through the positive 'green' adjective as well as the 'burden' of 'her eggs'. However, using 'burden' to describe the joy of nature's procreative powers already suggests the dark tone of the poem, a tone amplified by the turtle having to lay her eggs 'in their nest of sickness'. The traumatic destruction of nature is captured in 'the long migrations and the slow dying' of the 'restless wader' and all those suffocating in 'the stink of anger'. The aggressive sonics of 'stink', with its intense plosive T and fierce fricative K, capture the fury of Clarke's protest.

Speak no evil

While the poem's end memorably conjures up a metaphorical death rattle for our planet, it also condemns the hollowness of political rhetoric that proclaims commitment to tackling climate change as well as those who proclaim to protect global peace. It is curious that Clarke would actually lament 'vengeance', but it may be the case that she can only lament it simply because it is too late for vengeance to be possible or be important – only survival is important, anything else is a luxury in this new world where 'the sun [is] put out' and the entire planet 'burnt'. Read in this way, not only does the end of the poem point out the danger of inflammatory political rhetoric [see George W. Bush's 'You're either with us or against us' mantra] but also its futility. Only 'the ashes of language' are left, which suggests that language is much too flimsy a thing to bring about the changes necessary to reverse this seemingly unstoppable slide into global chaos. Instead meaningful action is what's needed. And even that may be enough as proved by the one million people who protested in London against Britain's involvement in the 2003 Invasion of Iraq.

However, despite the seeming uselessness of language at the end of the poem, its existence is ultimately a symbol of protest, of voicing anger at immoral actions. And maybe that's why it's worth lamenting – language and communication are the only things we can use to overcome our differences and divine a collective path to a more globally responsible existence. The poem then identifies both the danger and the destructiveness of language as well as its absolute necessity and power to broker a new future. God knows it's needed in times of religious extremism and dangerous alternative facts!

The sound of silence

For a poem that ends with language it is strangely silent. Rather than focusing upon the noise of the apocalypse Clarke plays it silently. The poem is dominated by visual imagery of struggling animal life, polluting oils slicks, fiery infernos and finally a smoke-filled nightmare. While all this imagery is memorably brought to life, it is the explosive presence of other sensory imagery that is most memorable.

Aural imagery in the poem is positioned curiously. The onomatopoeia of 'lap' is usually associated with the soothing repetitive rhythms of waves gently caressing the shore [as in W.B. Yeats' *The lake isle of Innisfree*] but here it seems much closer to 'slap' where the lapping of the sea is weighed down with the 'mortal stain' of oil and the ocean is given a greater heft both physically and sonically. The most significant aural moment in the poem comes with a seemingly irreversible action: 'the whale struck dumb by the missile's thunder'. Not only does the thunder carry with it a certain apocalyptic finality but it clearly shows nature's defeat in the face of awesome human technology. There is an irony here that we can find the technology to destroy the planet but not to save it. The terrible finality of 'the missile's thunder' is reinforced by Clarke's metre, where the predominantly iambic pattern is rearranged uniquely. Rather than the standard unstressed – stressed pattern, the line is loaded at the start by placing the use of a molossus [three successive stresses]. Let's put all that technical jargon into more straightforward visuals [stressed syllables are in bold]:

The **whale struck dumb** by the **miss** ile's **thun** der

It has a very strange effect where the molossus brings attention to the whale's incomprehension of what's happened and bringing our focus on the natural rather than the human action that causes it. It also causes an odd sonic effect like a boom followed by an aftershock that seems like a detonation at the start of the line.

However, such powerful sensory description is not just restricted to aural imagery. One of the most powerful words in the entire poem conjures up olfactory or smell imagery: 'stink'. The sonic power of that word has been discussed already, but here the word is used in a highly imaginative way. The 'stink' is the 'stink of anger' where the smell is conflated with emotion. How does anger smell then? Presumably not very nice at all, but who exactly is angry: the poet, the innocent  populace at large, the dying natural world? It's not clear and this ambiguity possibly makes the image even more effective. The end of the poem sees a similar conflation of the sensory with the emotional, except this time Clarke imposes tactile or touch imagery onto 'vengeance'. This is quite appropriate really as 'the scalded ocean and 'burnt earth evoke a sense of touch, conveying a world unbearably hot not capable of sustaining life of any type. However, by pairing this scalding with vengeance there is a suggestion that this is a type of divine vengeance, like God reigning down hellfire on humankind for its many sins. Even vengeance itself would seem exactly the right emotion to marry to this tactile imagery – a searing thirst for terrible revenge, a re-hot irrational rage suited to the cosmic injustice perpetrated by humankind's short-sightedness.

Crunchable *Lament* :

BURDEN – BREEDING – SICKNESS – SILK – IRIDESCENCE – SHADOW – STAIN – AHMED – FIRE – GUNSMITH – COMPANY – MUSIC – TURTLES – DOLPHIN – MISSILE'S – RESTLESS – DYING – STINK – BURNT – SCALDED – ASHES

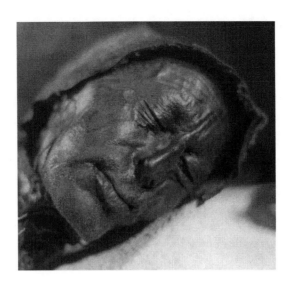

Seamus Heaney, *Punishment*

Love ties us together

The most striking first impression of Heaney's poem is its unusual shape on the page. The long[ish] sequence of 11 quatrains, together with the notably short lines, which range from two to eight syllables, give the impression of a compressed, dense flow of expression. In some ways the poem appears like the pressurised bog bodies that inspired the poem. In another more sinister connection to the poem the form resembles a rope, taut with tension between past and present, individual and collective, condemned and condemner, silence and voice. Unsurprisingly, the poem sees a number of oppositions interrogated by Heaney.

The lack of a rhyme scheme alongside the density of Heaney's observations [just look at all those nouns] makes each little quatrain surprisingly powerful. If it wasn't for the strong metre the poem would feel almost conversational and deeply personal. Heaney begins four of his eleven quatrains with the personal pronoun 'I', making it a deeply personal response. However, that strong personal voice is balanced by the notably silent 'you' of the bog body, who is imaginatively brought to life by Heaney before being even more imaginatively conflated with the present [or recent past of the Northern Irish civil conflict, The Troubles].

The body as object

While the metaphor of digging remains most strongly linked with Heaney's autobiographical early poetry, eerily, the digging in the poem seems more focused on the hidden bringing itself to the surface as opposed to a deliberate excavation. While the bog body is presented as passive the past that comes with it takes on a much more active role. Heaney challenges the utopian view of History as teaching us to avoid the mistakes of the past by suggesting that no such lessons of improvement have been learned. Instead, European cultures are trapped in cycles of brutal tribal violence that destroy individual freedoms. Writing in 1973, and attacked by some critics as presenting a simplistic and pessimistic view of cultural conflict, the subsequent conflicts over the past 40 years have proven Heaney depressingly accurate.

However, Heaney firstly chooses to personalise the past by focusing on the victim. The description here is quite sensual in capturing the vulnerability of the bog body, suddenly exposed to the elements once again. Empathetically, the speaker 'can feel [...] the wind / on her naked front' and the description of how the wind 'shakes the frail rigging / of her ribs' emphasises further the fragility of the body. Heaney also uses gentle alliteration of soft r-sounds together with the brittle short i-sounds in 'rigging and 'ribs' to create a sense of delicacy. This crafting of soundscapes is reflective of a wider strategy in the beginning stages of the poem. The first two stanzas are full of subtle sound patterns where a proliferation of soft n-, l- and s- sounds are subtly snagged on harsher fricatives and plosives. For instance, the n-sounds of 'can', 'nape', 'neck', 'wind', 'naked', 'front', 'nipples' are counteracted by the k-sounds in 'neck', 'naked' and 'shake'. This conflict in sound connects to the wider issues of conflict within the poem.

The sensual alliteration becomes increasingly erotic as the poem slides from neck to breasts [and further down] like a lover. The intimacy creates an

95

uncomfortable atmosphere and the poem has drawn much feminist fire for its eroticising and objectification of the female form. It could be argued that the patriarchal tribal injustice that killed this woman in the past is matched by a similarly male reception in the present through the speaking voice's objectifying observations. Objectification emphasising the fragility and weakness of the female can also be seen later in the poem where Heaney describes the 'brain's exposed / and darkened combs' and the 'muscles' webbing'.

Crime scene

The sensuality signalled by 'I can feel' at the start gives way to a greater objectivity as the voice becomes more scientific in its archaeological observations, almost as if describing a crime scene. This change is again signalled sonically with a slowing down of the short lines through long, broad vowel sounds, such as. 'dr<u>ow</u>ned', 'w<u>eigh</u>ing' and 'b<u>oughs</u>'. Furthermore, the observations move from the particularities of the female body to the environment that housed it all this time. Mention of 'the weighing stone', however, re-introduces the sinister suggestions of murder [previously suggested by 'halter'] that can be easily forgotten in the sensuality of the opening.

The fusion of body with bog is suggested by Heaney when he describes the woman as 'a barked sapling / that is dug up'. Here 'barked' describes the colouration of the body while 'sapling' describes her youth. The sound combinations of this phrase manage to capture the simultaneous brittleness yet great durability of the body. The crackling fricative of 'barked' runs both with and against the more elastic suppleness of 'sapling'.

Such skilful sculpting of sounds reappears in the final line of this quatrain where Heaney's description is most compressed. Like the great pressure of material pressing down on these bog bodies, the phrase 'oak-bone, brain-firkin' condenses meaning down to the absolute minimum words necessary. The power of this line can be seen in its relentless four sequential stressed beats [**oak-bone, brain-fir** kin]. Heaney uses hyphenation to fuse bog to body and surrounds the subject with a casing of objects. The 'bone' and 'brain' of this woman are enveloped imaginatively by 'oak' and 'firkin' – both wooden. 'Firkin' is one of those typically Anglo-Saxon sounding words that Heaney is fond of in his poetry. It's a small wooden vessel for storing butter and here is used to describe the woman's skull, which becomes literally a brain container. The sound patterns contained in this most condensed poetic line are impressive. Not only does Heaney employ assonance through the broad vowels of 'oak-bone' he links the 'bone, brain' through alliteration and the 'brain-firkin' through consonance of the r- and n-sounds. The overall impression is of a phrase meshing opposing concepts together through several sonic strands.

Love or hate crime?

The concept of love is disturbingly introduced into the poem via the noose around the woman's neck, which Heaney describes as 'a ring // to store / the memories of love'. This extraordinary equation of the noose and the wedding ring conflates murder and love, which allows the poem to reveal its central preoccupation: the collective 'punishment' of inappropriate love. Here the poem reveals the bog body as a 'little adulteress' who becomes a 'scapegoat' for the 'tribal, intimate revenge' of straying from expected norms. The conflict between the individual and the collective is revealed in the phrase 'before they punished you' where the faceless 'they' are subtly denigrated by the adjectives associated with the dead woman: 'little' and 'poor'. The fact that Heaney describes this woman as 'under-nourished' also reinforces her victimisation and prompts our pity.

The 'little adulteress' is alone; there is no male counterpart to be found, suggesting that only she was punished. Describing this woman as a 'poor scapegoat' further emphasises the unjust brutality of her treatment, implying her punishment was very much public, a chastening deterrent to further transgressive behaviour. However, Heaney is not content for us to sympathise with this victim of ancient pagan brutality. Cleverly he connects her to the time of composition [early 1970s Northern Ireland] through the description of her 'tar-black face'. In the Northern Irish Troubles the Irish Republican Army [I.R.A.] publicly humiliated any Catholic women caught fraternising with members of the British army.

These women were 'cauled in tar' and 'wept by the railings' with the reference to 'tar' explicitly connecting them to the 'tar-black' face of the 'little adulteress'. Heaney's verbification of the noun 'caul' is brilliantly appropriate and sinister:

'Caul' can mean close fitting woman's cap, but can also refer to where a new-born baby's head is covered by a part of the amniotic sac. Either way it denotes the tar cap forced on these women but also connotes a terrible corruption of the innocent and defenceless. However, Heaney complicates such a straightforward reading when he describes them as 'your betraying sisters'. Clearly, it is another explicit equation of past and present female victims, but this is made problematic by the adjective 'betraying' as this suggests wrongdoing and guilt rather than victimisation and innocence. There is an implied criticism of the women's looking for love in all the wrong places. There is also a suggestion of the vindictiveness of such 'tribal' justice with Heaney implying that these women [ancient and modern] are punished because they are 'beautiful' – a source of female power over men.

Peeping Tom?

This complication of the relationship between male observer and female observed dominates the end of the poem. We are not given a straightforward moral warning about male oppression of natural female desires. The complex, conflicted responses of the male speaker to the silent female is continued in the assertion that 'I almost love you'. The possessive pronoun reinforces the power of the individual male speaker and the fact that he can only 'almost love' her prevents a simple presentation of the speaker as moral crusader. In fact, he is much less than a voice of moral outrage. Instead the poet portrays himself an 'artful voyeur'; a sort of artistic peeping tom, who gains power from observation, but not through interaction or intervention. Heaney admits his cowardliness when he proclaims that he 'would have cast, I know / the stones of silence'. This allusion to biblical stories of stoning, particularly Mary Magdalene for adultery, introduces another male-voiced narrative that considers collective punishment of individual female wrongdoers. However, the fact that Christ prevents such brutality in this story slyly suggests another way forward... especially for a group supposed to be living by the teachings of Christ. A deep irony is presented by Heaney in the discrepancy between Catholic doctrine and Catholic nationalist behaviour.

The weakness of the individual in the face of collective power is shamefully described in the discrepancy between moral lip service and practical bravery.

 Heaney describes how he would 'connive / in civilised outrage / yet understand the exact /and tribal, intimate revenge'. The artist would ultimately ignore this brutal victimisation of vulnerable young women through a type of hollow outrage. The terrible thing about this is that he is unable to make any meaningful gestures because he understands *too well* the logic behind such brutality. When he proclaims he has 'stood dumb' it creates a sense of self-loathing that captures the difficulties of making an individual protest in the face of collective actions. In one sense, actually writing such a poem makes the type of meaningful protest that many individuals are unable to make in reality. The artist ultimately says the things that the individual cannot.

There are multiple conflicts in Heaney's dark, disturbing and complex poem:

There is the obvious conflict between the woman and the society that punished her; this parallels conflicts in contemporary Northern Ireland, such as that between the IRA and the British; there is also a psychological conflict within Heaney as witness to brutality, a conflict in his feelings towards this body and what it represents. And, we too, may be conflicted by the poem, unnerved by the way the naked female body is objectified by the male poet.

Crunchiment:

FEEL – HALTER – NECK – NAKED – NIPPLES – BEADS – FRAIL – RIBS – DROWNED – BOG – WEIGHING – RODS – UNDER – SAPLING – DUG – FIRKIN – SHAVED – BLACK – BLINDFOLD – NOOSE – STORE – MEMORIES – ADULTERESS – PUNISHED – FLAXEN-HAIRED – TAR-BLACK – SCAPEGOAT – ALMOST – CAST – SILENCE – VOYEUR – EXPOSED – DARKENED – WEBBING – BONES – DUMB – BETRAYING – CAULED – WEPT – CONNIVE – CIVILISED – UNDERSTAND – TRIBAL

John Agard, *Flag*

A sense of simplicity

Agard's opening is abrupt, confrontational, and immediately establishes the repetitive patterns that will define this poem. 'What's that' sits in a tonal register that feels out of place in a poem – the poetic register being one that we would normally associate with heightened, more formal language – and presents a directness that is disarming to the reader in the first instance. Suggesting urgency, a demand for an answer in a very short time frame, it cocks the reader's ears; something's happening, and it's happening now.

This makes 'fluttering' all the more intriguing as the poem's third word. 'Fluttering' sits within that register that we naturally assume to be more 'poetic' – rightly or otherwise. It also, almost literally, flutters. Though no clear metrical pattern of stresses has been established – nor, indeed, is ever really clearly established during the poem – the triplet trailing away from the initial stressed syllable at the start of 'flú-tter-ing' seems to flutter in and of itself; a world away from the two stressed syllables that are the most obvious way to enunciate the 'What's that' that opens the poem.

As the second line of the poem begins, Agard's conceit – the central idea or notion that guides a poem or text – becomes clearer. The question is established at the start of the very short, three-line stanza – 'What's that fluttering in the breeze?' – and is then supposedly answered in the following two lines. So just as the informal register of 'What's that' was immediately noteworthy, so the elision of 'it' and 'is' to create the colloquial 'It's' is noteworthy as the second line offers a seemingly offhand answer, 'It's just a piece of cloth'. These two lines, concluding the poem's first stanza, run along in an effortless way because of their metrical construction. These lines can be very easily, comfortably read as iambs – pairs of syllables where the first is unstressed and the second is stressed, such as in the word 'today'. As such, 'It's just a piece of cloth / that brings a nation to its knees' rolls easily off the tongue in one seamless unit, with stresses falling equidistant from one another, more often than not on monosyllabic words – 'just', 'piece', 'cloth', 'brings', 'na-', 'to', 'knees'.

The words 'knees' at the end of the third line – concluding the poem's first stanza – sets up a rhyme scheme for the poem as a whole. The first and third [final] lines of each stanza rhyme, broadly speaking, with the second line of each stanza adrift on its own, relative to the stanza considered as a discrete unit. Such a structure makes each stanza seem compact, self-contained, and almost twee. The rhyme at the end of the third line becomes expected, and the final line builds up towards it only to land with the predictable thud of the punny punchline of a bad dad joke. This is much the same effect as the sing-song iambic structure of the first stanza's second two lines creates – 'It's just a piece of cloth / that brings a nation to its knees' doesn't sound particularly serious, because the metre makes it tick along so easily towards the pathos of that rhyme.

This structure continues throughout the first four stanzas of the poem, creating a sense of simplicity; a structure is established which creates almost sing-song stanzas, and then that structure repeats in similarly bundled units.

As such, 'fluttering in the breeze' becomes 'unfurling from a pole', which then transitions to 'rising over the tent', before coming to 'flying across a field'. The structure remains the same: there's a gerund – an '-ing' form of a verb, such as 'flying' or 'fluttering' – followed by a preposition construction of some type to place the action – 'from a', 'in the', 'across a', 'over the' – and then a simple noun – 'breeze', 'pole', 'tent', 'field'.

The final line of each stanza replicates itself in a similarly predictable way. Each iteration of the final line begins with 'that', launches into a verb – 'brings', 'makes', 'dares', 'will outlive' – with a subject – 'a nation', 'the guts of men', 'the coward', 'the blood'. It's a little like a book teaching a child how to read; it doesn't automatically seem like what poetry is *supposed* to be.

The final stanza does offer a breath of fresh air, relatively speaking. The repetitive structure of the opening question of each stanza changes, so 'What's that' goes out the window and is replaced by 'How can I'. There is clearly some kind of change or pivot here. The focus turns from over there – 'that' – to over here – 'I'. But once again the explanatory voice fills up the last two stanzas of the verse – the colloquialism of 'it's' continues in the familiarity of 'my friend', and any metrical quirks of the line 'Just ask for a flag my friend' are nicely ironed out in the soothing iambs of 'then blind your conscious to the end'.

Like a flag

It is tempting to get to this point in John Agard's text and think that it is a simple work, barely worthy of any serious, devoted literary study. We might struggle, for instance, to write much about the presentation of conflict in the poem or about its atmosphere. This, however, is not the full picture. Though in terms of vocabulary, syntax and structure the poem seems simple, it is, in fact riddled with teasing possibilities for double meanings, layers of sense, and patterns that hold greater significance than they seem to at first. In fact, a poem that means lots of things all at once and has patterns that look simple but are very significant is rather a lot like a flag in and of itself.

These patterns are vital to understanding what *Flag* is trying to do as a piece of literature. The establishment of such a clear structure from stanza to stanza invites more complex thought about changes within that structure, growth and development as each stanza to the next, and the overarching direction of the text.

With this in mind, it's worth thinking about the ending of each line in the entire poem. It is common to speak of masculine line endings and feminine line endings – where 'masculine' endings are those that land on a long or stressed syllable, like 'to-**day**', and 'feminine' endings are those that finish on any number of short or unstressed syllables, like '**mut**-tering'. Every single line ending in *Flag* has a 'masculine' line ending. The majority are monosyllabic –

with the sole exception of 'relent' – and almost all end, at least when spoken out loud, in a consonant, or consonantal sound. The field of battle is – or has been – so overtly masculine for so much of its history, with women only recently given anything resembling fully equal status as part of the armed forces in this country. Such linguistic macho-macho behaviour is clearly deliberate.

In a structure that repeats itself, with the choice word for each linguistic 'gap' to be filled seeming like a mere act of replacement, the words themselves become a pattern. So while the repetitive nature of the first line of each of the first four stanzas seems dull – 'What's that' over and again – it establishes a set of boundaries that become significant. In this instance, it's the verbs that do the important work; as the poem progresses, they grow more confident, more headstrong, more combative. 'Fluttering', the nervous, fading-away triplet of the first stanza, holds its head a little higher, imbued with a certain

104

muted grandeur as it becomes 'unfurling'. The stress has moved from the anxious spot of the first of three syllables – whereby the rest of the word dies away into nothingness – to occupy the middle of the word, the centre of the room at the party. 'Unfurling' therefore has a poise and stature that a verb like 'fluttering' cannot have by its phonological nature; it just doesn't *sound* as good. 'Rising' goes a step further – the unnecessary fuss of a third syllable is cut out, and the low, stodgy vowel sound of 'uh' – both in 'fluttering' and in 'unfurling' – is tuned up a notch, to the more full, complex diphthong in 'I' – the 'rising' has a sophisticated kind of curvature to it. By the time this pattern reaches 'flying' – it's basically taking flight.

The same is true of the questions themselves. Even the progression from the question word 'what' to the question word 'how' is important: 'How' is the more complex, sophisticated question, an intellectual step up from the mere 'what' that dominates the first four stanzas. Through establishing such seemingly simple and repetitive structures Agard draws our attention to the subtle but vital distinction between those two ways of asking.

Agard's use of double meanings are also a key complexity introduced into what sets itself up to be a deliberately, and misleadingly, simple poem. Perhaps the most fundamental word, repeated in each of the first four stanzas, is, ironically, 'piece'. The 'piece' of cloth that is identified in each of the four stanzas – and that same 'piece' that is the subject of 'How can I possess' ['possess', of course, being dangerously closed to the idea of 'being possessed' by some demon or external force] in the final stanza – is an important choice of word. Not only does it obviously represent an item, a physical bit of the cloth that comprises a flag, symbolically it is also part of something larger. The word 'piece' evokes a more substantial whole – just as a 'piece' of cake implies that there is a larger cake from which the piece has been extracted. Fundamentally, the whole idea of a flag that Agard is hinting at throughout this poem is the idea of something bigger than an individual, or than the two individuals having some sort of dialogue in this poem – it refers to something that stretches beyond the literal and the fabric reality of any 'piece of cloth' and points to a grander ideal. In that sense, 'piece' is crucial;

it's part of a larger structure.

Perhaps more obviously, though, 'piece' seems to make an ironic, almost knowing joke in the form of a pun. Flags, very often, and in this poem in particular, are seen more prominently in battle – during times of war, when the poem's bodily language of 'blood' and 'guts' and 'knees' really comes into play. As such, 'piece' at least partially must call to mind 'peace' – a homophone that means something very different and is spelled differently, too. While 'a peace of cloth' might be all the peoples of the world united under one common flag, a 'piece' of cloth both again draws attention to the fractured small part of a larger whole, and suggests that this fracturing in and of itself sows the seeds for division to be inevitable – 'peace' doesn't come in 'pieces'.

'Just' is used throughout the poem in an apparently nonchalant manner. It's 'just' a piece of cloth, we're told, and if you want such a cloth you 'just' have to ask for it. It's nothing – 'just' get one. Again, the context of conflict, wars, and flags adds further meaning to the word 'just'. Not only do we have to consider the concept of 'justice' – and when 'justice' is seen to have failed, creating conflict between what is technically right and what feels fair – but we have to give credence to the notion of a 'just war'. A philosophical concept with intense scholarship behind it dating back thousands of years, a 'just war' can seem like an oxymoron, but is a  crucial part of the way different nations – thus, people with different flags – interact with each other in our own world. The excessive, repetitive use of 'just' in its more colloquial context, to mean 'merely' or 'only', serves to belittle its weightier meanings – of justice and the proper and proportionate way to engage in war and violence when all other options have been exhausted.

The last line of the entire poem contains two multi-faceted words that are at the apex of how Agard uses specific words to hint at the larger significance of his poem. The expectation, having talked about the physicality of the 'cloth' of the flag 'fluttering in the breeze', and so on, would be to talk about the need to 'bind' something 'to the end' of it – as in, fix, fasten, tie on. Instead, Agard gives us 'blind', which seems both totally inadequate and bewildering. Rather than 'binding' your conscience to it – fastening your conscience, securing it – Agard's instruction is to '*blind* it' – make it vulnerable in its lack of sight and insight, vision, context, sense. The idea of 'blinding' conscience also pervades through to 'to the end', the poem's three final words. Whereas 'bind your conscience to the end' might open itself to a more literalist interpretation – the verb implying literally tying something to one end of the flagpole – 'blind' suggests an alternative meaning. On a poetical level, 'the end' is the end of the poem, while on the literal level, it does still refer to the end of the flagpole, the physical point that rides highest above the government office or public building, or that flies high above the heads of soldiers readying for battle. On the more metaphorical level, though, 'the end' represents 'wit's end' – the point where the human capacity for critical reasoning and thinking for oneself are passed over in favour of mindless patriotism and order obeying; or 'the end' to mean the point where the final breaths of a human life might seem closer than they did before.

Agard's poem seems simple, but is deceptive. By establishing very clear-cut, simple, repetitive structures and forms, the poet invites closer scrutiny. When the time is taken to let the patterns, tricks, and double meanings emerge, Agard's work – which can be seen to take conflict and war a little too lightly on first reading – becomes a little darker and a little more complicated. Certainly, through the metonym of the flag as 'just a piece of cloth' the poet debunks ideas of patriotism in a memorable way.

Flag crushed:

FLUTTERING – CLOTH – NATION – WHAT'S – JUST – GUTS – TENT – PIECE – COWARD – FIELD – JUST – OUTLIVE – POSSESS – FLAG – BLOOD

Jo Shapcott, *Phrase Book*

Lost in the action

On a first and, in fact, on subsequent readings this is a very confusing poem. It's hard to work out what's actually going on, even at a basic level. We do learn that the speaker is an English woman and she's talking as if to us, as if we are there in the scene and she thinks we might be able to help her somehow. Clearly too she needs this help. But where she is and what precisely is happening to her is difficult to pin down. The first stanza is immediately disorientating and disturbing. In the second line a 'Human Remains Pouch' [HRP] is mentioned, which sounds like an official military term for a body bag, i.e. something a corpse is put in, perhaps on a battlefield. Why, we instantly wonder, will this woman's 'skin' 'do' for a body bag and why only 'for a moment'? Does she mean that she feels dead inside her skin? What will happen after that moment? Two lines into the poem and the reader is already unsettled. And alarmed. Two swift, contradictory imperatives follow: 'Look down there/ up here' and 'Quickly. Slowly'. The imperative form combined with the shortness of the lines conveys urgency, but we don't know what we're meant to be looking at or why we need to look at it. We don't know either whether she's contradicting herself, changing her mind from one moment to the next, or whether this is a sequence of commands and we are meant first to look up then down, quickly and then slowly. And, of course, no explanation follows.

In pieces

Look at the poem on the page and it seems fairly orderly and conventional. Nine solid-enough seeming stanzas, each arranged in the familiar-looking pattern of a quatrain. Look down the right hand side of the page, however, and the edge of the poem looks rather uneven, erratic and jagged. Moreover,

inside the outer semblance of order there is disorder and fragmentation. For instance, three caesuras break up the first stanza and the last line of the stanza is incomplete, running over the end of the stanza and into the second one. Also, no regular metre or rhyme scheme keeps

things in any sort of harmonious shape or holding pattern. Furthermore, the subject jumps about to such an extent that the poem's almost incoherent. Not only is the narrative broken into fragments, it's also disjointed: What, for example, links the comments in the first sentence to the injunction to 'look'? How do these instructions connect to the last bit of information, 'this is my own front room'? We have a setting, at least, a domestic one, but why didn't the speaker establish that first? If she's in her own home, why the reference to the HRP? It's all really rather distressingly disorientating. It's not the woman, we might think, but the reader who's in need of the right phrase book to interpret what's really going on here.

No sooner have we learnt that the woman is in her 'front room' than our purchase on what's going on is loosened by the next line telling us that she is also 'lost in action' and 'live from a war'. How can she be in her own room and simultaneously lost in action in a war? The reference to a 'screen' suggests that either she might be watching news coverage of a war and is 'lost' in this experience, or that, perhaps, she's a war reporter - but then how she in her own room? This stanza travels along as bewildering lines as the first. We might echo the woman's 'I don't understand you' by saying we don't understand her either. We are addressed directly, asked questions, but have no idea of possible answers. We are told we 'are right' and then instantly that we 'are wrong'. Okay, about what? 'Things are going well,' she tells us. Really? Or perhaps the reverse ['badly']. What things are these that are either going well or badly? In what way are they going either well or badly? When we reach the last line of this stanza we're likely to agree, and be inclined to respond by shouting YES, YOU ARE DISTURBING ME. Hence Shapcott generates and sustains a jittery atmosphere, a jangled feeling of unease.

Despite the confused and confusing, fragmentary and disjointed narrative, a few things, however, soon begin to come clearer:

1. The poem is a dramatic monologue in the voice of an unnamed Englishwoman. And the situation she's in appears to be dramatic and distressing

2. She is, or thinks she is, in her front room, but somehow feels 'lost' in the action of a war. Hence the use of the military jargon, such as HRP.

3. She's not making much sense - her line of thought is impossible to follow; it leaps from one thing to another in non-sequiturs. She contradicts herself almost immediately

4. The woman is speaking to us as if we were there in the room with her. She seems to understand as little about us as we do about her

5. As the title suggests, the poem appears to be something to do with miscommunication or the difficulty of communicating, particularly in extreme circumstances.

So, so far, the poem is a bit like a shattered mosaic. With have bits and  pieces of a story, a character and a situation, but we can't put the whole thing together, yet. If you're familiar with artistic and literary movements, the poem's fragmentary and disjointed style might set you thinking of Modernism or perhaps of a Cubist painting, such as Juan Gris's painting of a guitar. Although it's addressed to a listener, certainly Shapcott's poem has a lot in common with a favourite narrative technique of Modernist novelists, the stream of consciousness.

The third stanza confirms that the woman has been watching coverage of a war on her television. We seem to be on solider ground now. Again she refers to military terminology 'bliss' and again there's a focus on communication or lack of it, 'please write it down'. As the poem proceeds, the irony of the military use of the acronym 'bliss', to describe evasive action, is foregrounded by blending it with the woman's understanding of the word in a loving, erotic context, as a physical coming together, when she raised her 'body to his mouth'. We don't know who this new character, 'he', is, other than the fact that he was the woman's lover. The two narratives, of the pilots on TV and the lover in the room, become intertwined. Hence ominous-sounding military jargon 'Side-Looking Airborne Radar', the 'Kill Box', 'stealthed' and euphemisms for killed, such as 'cleansed' and 'Taken Out' mix uneasily and ironically with comments such as 'this is really beautiful'.

Once the woman realises that the pilots can fire rockets with 'Pinpoint Accuracy' she grows even more agitated. In the seventh stanza she seems on

the verge of evacuating her home, convinced that it is about to be targeted. She also appears to be addressing us, as if we are going to help her get out: 'There is another/ bag there' and then suddenly, alarmingly, she tells us to 'look out'. Of course, we have no idea what to be looking out for. And it's not clear whether she is even talking to us or to another character silent and invisible to us, but there in the room with her. While the narrator switches erratically between topics - the lover, love, fighter pilots, her belongings - we might consider possible explanations for her bizarre behaviour. Two or three present themselves, and you may be able to think of others:

1. The woman has lost her wits: The coverage of a foreign war she watches on her TV in her own home in England has made her imagine erroneously that she could be the victim of a precision strike by a fighter plane from a foreign war.

2. She is perfectly rational, but, highly agitated and distressed. She may be English, but lives in a foreign city where a war is raging. That might explain why she refers to not being understood and not understanding, 'please speak slowly'.

3. Perhaps we shouldn't read the poem in a literal way or treat it as a realist text. Perhaps to do so would be a category error. In fact, Shapcott is often considered to be a surrealist poet, deliberately blurring the boundaries in her work between reality, dreams and the imagination. Read through this perspective, in some surreal, nightmarish way the conflict has indeed migrated from the screen into this woman's domestic English world.

Let me pass please

We'll never know which of these interpretations is 'correct' and, in any case, this isn't a poem that deals in answers. In fact, it's fairly riddled with questions. They come thick and fast in the final stanza, six in just three lines. Some of the questions are incomplete, 'where can I find?' giving the impression that she is speaking urgently. Distressingly, the woman feels she must prove her innocence, 'I have done / nothing'. By placing us an addressee throughout the poem, Shapcott makes us feel like we should be able to do something to help and perhaps, even, that we are somehow implicated in this situation. But, of course, we are powerless to intervene. And, in the last lines, our presence, or that of our invisible counterpart in the poem takes on another more sinister dimension. Rather than being there to aid the woman, as she, and we, had assumed, suddenly it seems, we or this unseen other might actually be an enemy, perhaps even someone blocking her escape: 'Let me pass please'. If this is the case, the end of the poem becomes darker and more distressing.

Overall, however we read it, the poem implies that we are not as separated from the distant worlds we witness at one remove through the images on our television sets as we might like to think. In the poem the boundaries between different realities collapse. What happens on TV suddenly starts happening around the woman. Our seemingly secure world is actually far more vulnerable, Shapcott suggests, and conflict can come unexpectedly much closer to home and overturn our lives.

Jo Shapcott is a poet who specialises in dramatic monologues which present 'reality' from unusual and oblique perspectives. She has, for instance, written monologues in the voice of the cartoon cat, Tom, from *Tom and Jerry*, and in the voice of a cow infected with Mad Cow's Disease. As the poetry archive writes of her work, she is also 'particularly drawn to moments of dissolution when the boundaries between the self and the outside world are disrupted'[2] Combine the unusual perspectives with the dissolution of boundaries and we arrive at poems such as *Phrase Book*. In Shapcott's disorientating poetic world, readers and characters are in dire need of a phrase book that will help us make sense of a reality which often seems as if it is written in a foreign language.

Phrase Book crunched:

HERE – REMAINS – LOOK – ROOM – WAR – UNDERSTAND – YOU – DISTURBING – TV – BLEND – SLOWLY– BLISS – MOUTH – HE– PILOTS – CAUGHT J– -STARS – GENTEMAN – BEAUTIFUL – KILL– SCREENS – STEALTHED – OUT – HARMS – CASES – BAG – ENOUGH – EVASION – LOVE – POUNDING – DUST – CONSULATE– DO – WHAT – PLEASE

---

[2] http://www.poetryarchive.org/poet/jo-shapcott

Imtiaz Dharker, *Honour Killing*

honour killing
noun

the killing of a relative, especially a girl or woman, who is perceived to have brought dishonour on the family.

I have wanted to efface myself

With a mixed heritage and a mixed upbringing across Pakistan and Scotland Dharker is a film-maker, visual artist and poet who describes herself as a Scottish Muslim Calvinist who has married into Welshness. She belongs to a group of vocal and prolific female Indian writers to emerge after Indian independence, a group which includes Sujata Bhatt, Mamta Khalia and Tara Patel. At first *Honour Killing* seems to be about killings carried out against women in predominantly Muslim countries by another family member, usually male [it's thought that this poem was prompted for Dharker by a similar killing in Lahore], but as the poem develops, it becomes obvious that there are different forces at play. Multiple faiths are referenced and the speaker 'takes off' layers of their identity to reach nothingness - she even takes 'off this skin, / and then the face, the flesh'. Eventually she removes a key symbol of womanhood and potential motherhood, 'the womb'. In divesting herself of her womb, she removes one of the reasons behind honour killings, the dishonour brought about by children born out of wedlock. This stripping down of the physical self may be a liberation of the inner soul, but isn't it also a form of grimly determined and disturbingly intimate self-mutilation?

Conflicting themes

There are lots of conflicting themes in this poem, such as:

Freedom vs. entrapment	The speaker of the poem says that she has 'no choice' in wearing 'this black coat of a country', yet she has the freedom to take off the clothes she no longer wants to wear
Keeping vs. losing your identity	The speaker erases her social identity in order to create a new one and find a 'new geography'
Losing vs. finding a voice	The speaker says that the symbols of religion have taken away her 'choice' and made her 'faithless', and most particularly 'muffled my own voice'. Conversely, by writing this poem the speaker is finding and asserting that very same voice that has been taken away

Unpeeling the self

The speaker 'undresses' throughout the poem, taking off the outer layer first, the 'black coat', then the 'black veil', then the 'silks'. In the first three stanzas it's just the physical clothes that are taken off. But from halfway through, at the fourth stanza, the speaker uses the same neutral, painless-sounding verb to describe '*taking* off this skin, / and then the face, the flesh, the womb', as if this is just as easy as removing clothes. After removing these increasingly intimate layers the speaker wants to discover a new identity: 'Let's see / what

I am in here / when I squeeze past / the easy cage of bone'. So body parts, such as the skin, face, flesh and womb are treated as if they were 'clothes'. This is significant because up until this point in the poem the layers being taken off were man-made and artificial, and, of course, particularly indicated cultural and religious identity. Perhaps the poet is saying that a 'womb' is comparable to another piece of clothing, one that, through making her a woman, defines her and pushes her into a lower position in society.

Once all this undressing has happened the speaker feels able and free to look back outwards to the world. She wants to know where things stand now that all the obvious symbols of society's influence have gone: 'Let's see / what I am in here' and 'Let's see / what I am out here'. Notice the subtle difference between 'in here' and 'out here'- the poem turns around at this last stanza to peek outwards from 'the easy cage of bone' towards a new world, a 'new geography'. The implication is that changing herself the speaker also changes the world.

Colours/objects

An accomplished visual artist, Dharker is a very painterly poet. Creating vivid images that are very direct, she makes use of symbolism and images to make her words come to life. There are, however, with all symbols, lots of different potential readings.

1. 'At last I'm taking off this coat' - This could be referring to a chador [a long black garment worn by Muslim women, leaving only the face exposed] However, one could also argue that since Dharker much more obviously refers to religious symbols elsewhere in the poem, like the 'veil' and the 'silks', this is a more culturally neutral and universal image

2. 'I'm taking off this veil' - The 'veil' is pretty clearly a Muslim headscarf. But, interestingly, the poet very specifically makes it a 'black veil', which has undertones of mourning and grief

3. 'gave my god a devil's face' - The word 'god' is specifically not capitalised. God is normally capitalised in religions with only one God, as in both Christianity and Islam. However, the pronoun 'my', along with the decapitalisation of 'god', signals this isn't a typical god - it's a personal one and possibly one that doesn't belong to a major religion. Or alternatively, the non-specific god again universalises the experience. This supports the theme of religion in the poem, which is certainly non-specific in terms of not being 'about' any one religion

4. 'I'm taking off these silks' - These silks are indicated to be Hindu, since they appear in the same stanza as 'the mangalsutra', a necklace tied around a bride's neck by her groom in Hindu cultures to identify her as a married woman. Perhaps silks also have connotations of women dancing for men's enjoyment, reinforced by the reference to 'feed dictator dreams'

5. 'making, crafting, / plotting / at my new geography' - The metaphor of maps and map reading conveys the formative influence of place on identity and suggests that finding a new identity is like discovering a new country. At the end of the poem there is a hopeful sense that new things will be found after the last stanza has finished.

Destruction vs. liberation

The title of this poem suggests the ending of a life and therefore destruction. The images of removing parts of the body would certainly support that. The euphemistic verb in 'I'm taking off this skin' cannot disguise how horribly painful such as process would be. The speaker may have been 'beggared' by her marriage, but the form of the poem suggests a whittling down, a reducing of the self. The particular emphasis on anatomical body parts, such as 'the easy cage of bone', the 'skin', 'the face, the flesh, / the womb', breaks down the speaker's identity as if it's in a science textbook. It's as if her body is external and incidental to a speaker who is immune to its pain and immune to feelings of loss. This disembodiment supports the theme of questioning identity, since our overall impression of the speaker is that they cease to be human. The focus on the female body in parts might make us think of the 'lover's blazon', a convention from Renaissance literature in which a male lover praises their beloved through describing various bits of her body. If we have this in mind, we can see that Dharker empowers her female speaker; by divesting herself of the sort of attractive physical features admired by men she escapes male attempts to control of her identity.

However, even though the speaker shows the breaking apart and dismantling identity, the last stanza indicates that once everything has been taken away the speaker has a blank state from which she can start to reconstruct herself on her own terms. Once she has got rid of everything that is associated with society and religion she can start 'making, crafting, / plotting / at my new geography', and can emerge to 'see / what I am out here'. The speaker is not reduced by the transformative process; the poem's narrowing form actually embodies a purifying and concentrating of the essence of her selfhood. Notice that subversive verb, 'plotting'. It suggests that this speaker may be planning some sort of revenge on men who seek to control women's lives through the brutal and barbaric convention of honour killings. Watch Dharker's unflinching reading her own poem and you'll pick up this note of defiance and challenge: https://www.youtube.com/watch?v=M04_yMEoecE

Honour Killing crunched:

COAT – COUNTRY – HABIT – CHOICE – VEIL – FAITH – DEVIL – SILKS – DICTATOR – MANGALSUTRA – RINGS – SKIN – FACE – FLESH – WOMB – CAGE – BONE – PLOTTING – GEOGRAPHY

NB

Another way in which Dharker's poem can be seen as being about the experience of all women and not just those oppressed by honour killings is the way it echoes the ideas and imagery of the work of Sylvia Plath. Plath's poetry repeatedly features images of a female character stripping off outer layers of identity, for instance, in a bid to find a freer, truer, purer self within. Often in her poetry this inner self seeks escape from patriarchal forces that shape and constrict the outer identity. For a taste of this, perhaps you might like to read her extraordinary poem *Ariel*. Such intertextuality implies we could read Dharker's *Honour Killing* as a fundamentally feminist poem.

INDIA

Sujata Bhatt, *Partition*

Breaking apart

The partition of India in 1947 saw the majority-Muslim parts of British India split off from the bulk of the country, which was mostly Hindu. These two areas were called the Dominion of India and the Dominion of Pakistan when they were still under the rule of the British Empire, and the partition coincided with both areas becoming independent states. The idea for a geographic split of the country was devised by Lord Louis Mountbatten, who was the last Viceroy of India, and resulted in the creation of East Pakistan [today Bangladesh] and West Pakistan [today's Pakistan], with the republic of India in between them. Partition was devastating. The creation of quasi-sectarian, religiously determined states led to the displacement of roughly 12million people, creating a vast refugee crisis that spawned violent conflict. Estimates of how many people died during the course of partition vary between a few hundred thousand and two million. Sujata Bhatt's poem sketches a tiny piece of this narrative through the narrow framework of three female characters, the speaker, her mother and her mother's aunt.

Now and then

The most important word in the first line is 'then'. Crucially, this is a poem fixated on - and unable to escape from - the past. 'Then', also, is a fundamentally othering word; it separates a 'then' from a 'now' in much the same way as we separate a 'them' from an 'us'. This first line of Sujata Bhatt's poem contextualises its narrative - the first word 'she' makes the reader aware both of a female voice that will be central to this narrative, but also of some kind of speaker of the poem; somebody who might become an 'I' as the poem progresses.

The pronouns in this opening section of the poem – which cannot be divided into stanzas as it flows freely as one continuous unit – feel incessant. 'She was nineteen-years-old', 'she stood in her garden', 'she could hear', 'she felt' – the deliberate avoidance of a name, or any other means of identifying the poem's main figure seems deliberate. The effect is a kind of distancing – both removing the 'she' from the speaker of the poem, and thus the reader, in making 'her' unidentifiable and vague despite the specific details of the situation, and removing the 'she' of the past from the 'she' of the present who is more clearly identified later on in the poem.

Despite the structure of the poem – which is functionally free verse in one long, undivided stanza that covers the entire text – Bhatt uses stress patterns to emphasise and draw attention to key moments in the narrative. The first three lines are dominated by suggestions of a lilting triple rhythm that feels informal and conversational – removed from a laboured poetic register of rhythm. The three-beat units of 'nineteen-years', 'stood in her', and 'cries of the' form the core of the first three lines, and after the jarring 'masculine' line ending of the first line which draws attention to 'then', placing the text in the past, the 'feminine' endings on 'garden', 'people' and 'station' all relax metrical tension, meaning the ends of lines don't stand out, obviously setting up a poetic structure of cut-off lines. 'Their noise' again creates a heavier ending, and the spondee, two stresses one after the other, on 'new sound', is, literally, a new sound, emphasised by the three unstressed syllables in the middle of 'added to the city', the end of that line.

Even the birds sounded different

Partition is a poem intensely concerned with space, and the politics of that space. The focus can be detected early on, when the figure in the poem 'stood in her garden' – the possessive pronoun of *'her* pronoun' is clearly important – particularly when contrasted with 'the people / stranded in the Ahmedabad railway station'. Whereas *her* garden is a possessed space with

no clear limits or boundaries, the 'Ahmedabad railway station', where people are 'stranded' and confined in a space that is clearly not theirs – it is named, civic, pertaining to no individual.

Ahmedabad itself is a city in the north-western state of Gujarat in India, and historically saw intense difficulty during the partition of India in 1947. Violence erupted between Hindus – many of whom settled in Ahmedabad from Pakistan – and Muslims – many of whom fled from Gujarat into nearby Pakistan.

As the poem goes on, though, that garden space comes to feel more confining. While 'her aunt' would 'go to the station everyday / with food and water' to help the refugees, the poem's central figure – the speaker's mother – 'felt afraid, / felt she could not go with her aunt'. Repetition of 'felt' reinforces the feeling of being trapped by her fear, so by the time the text returns to 'so she stood in the garden / listening', that space comes to feel much more limited, narrow, and restrictive. It is a garden whose atmosphere is suddenly transformed, like everything else by partition – 'even the birds sounded different' - a space taken over by unfamiliarity despite 'her' ownership of it, a space which changes to become 'the garden' in line 12. Though she seeks it under the shade of the trees, in this familiar, suddenly unfamiliar garden the mother can find no 'consolation'.

Repetition becomes key to narrowing that space even further. 'The cries of the people' in the third line are repeated in 'the cries of the people' in line 19; 'she stood in her garden' repeats to 'she stood in the garden' in line 12; 'go with her aunt' in line 11 repeats in line 17; 'and each day' in line 16 comes back just two lines later; even the 'listening' that begins line 13 echoes across to line 19. Though the cries of the people may be a 'new sound added to the city', it's a sound that becomes incessant, repeating itself and confining the space of the poem.

This verbal repetition pretty much stops after the poem's volta – or turn. The 'Now' that announces itself commandingly in line 20 is the pivot point of the text, clearly separating the past from the present, establishing a narrative over there and an interaction over here space once again defined and delineated. The female voice of the first half of the poem is now defined more clearly, as 'my mother', and is given her own space once again. While 'her garden' fell into 'the garden', the speaker's mother is clearly in 'her kitchen' – possessed space once more. Having had her narrative told by someone else on her behalf, the mother figure now speaks intimately in direct speech.

At this point, the poem also starts to manipulate and discuss space in its literal representation on the page. Typographically, lines 27 onwards are laid out in a deliberately challenging way – creating spaces at the beginnings of lines that vary in size, pushing the text back past a barrier of white space. In line 27, the effect is one of an emotional nostalgia. Though the quotation is unbroken from 'India was always there' to 'But how I wish I had / gone with my aunt', it's another world away. You can feel the pause, the uncertainty in her voice – the physical space even creates an audible thought process; a staring off into the distance out of the kitchen window. The lines themselves, displaced as they are, also get shorter here – the narrative becomes more uncertain, leaping across line divides in broken, jagged bites.

The next occurrence of this typographical unsettling is less clear. What does the gulf between 'I still feel' and 'guilty about that' mean in lines 30-31? Is it perhaps shame, looking back over fifty years to her failure to help out during the trauma and desperation of the partition of India? Or is it simply an uncertainty in and of itself, trying to work out what on earth it is you feel reflecting back on such a historic event on your doorstep? Again, the gap is contained with quotation marks, the direct speech of the speaker's mother in her kitchen, which again creates an impression of an audible gap in her speech; a moment of contemplation, frustration, or desperation. Perhaps there is even a suggestion that as she ages, her memory of the incident might be failing; the faltering shown in the physical gap on the page may be as much a grasping for the past as an active rewriting or reinterpreting of history through the contemporary expression of it.

Desperation and frustration are most certainly at the heart of the poem's ending, where the use of space comes to a head. 'How could they / have let a man / who knew nothing / about geography / divide a country?' the speaker's mother asks, with the closing quotation mark ending the text. For the first time, the spaces come in different sizes. The gap between 'they' and 'have' is a small gap, only a handful of characters' worth, but the distance between 'nothing' and 'about geography' is much bigger – about twice the size. This, of course, is the poem's own partition; a literal, visual representation of the wresting apart of space by those who do not have rightful ownership of it the men 'who knew nothing / about geography'.

This toying with the idea of space through the medium of physical gaps on the page shows what the poem is really interested in – the ownership of space. Women's voices dominate the poem – both in the female author of the text whose voice we assume to be the narrative speaker, and in her mother who is quoted in the text and who forms the subject of the narrative throughout. Men are almost entirely absent other than the blame they are portioned for the tragedy of partition – the men 'who knew nothing / about geography' – and in the way women are thought of in relation to them. And that's important – 'her aunt' is defined primarily as 'her father's sister', and for some reason that relational definition is deemed important. Crucially, though, women *seem* to own the spaces of this poem – to dominate the text, to stand in 'her garden' and 'her kitchen' looking out on the rest of the world – but can never fully have control over them. The two women stand in 'her kitchen' talking about 'they' – invariably, a male 'they' – and 'a man / who knew nothing'. Maleness invades that kitchen, the female space as defined by the two women talking in it. So, too, does it invade 'her garden', which becomes 'the garden' as the poem wears on after the mention of her aunt as being 'her father's sister'.

Colonial narratives of ownership are also clearly at play. No poetic discussion of the partition of India could possibly avoid an engagement with the politics of colonialism, and Bhatt's text is an open repudiation of it – the 'how could they' question that closes the poem is clearly a question that is asked in anger, frustration, and disbelief. Though the text has no clear metrical structure, this section is remarkable for the sheer breath of possibility when it comes to stress and diction. 'How could they' here could be read in almost any way: 'Hów could they', with only one emphasis; 'Hów coúld they', with the emphases in crescendo to 'could'; 'Hów coúld théy', with emphasis growing in frustration throughout; 'How coúld they', with a much harder  landing on 'could' to focus on the sheer arrogance of what 'they' did; 'How could théy', to reinforce the otherness of the people who inflicted this outside decision on India.

Bhatt's frustration at the scars that the partition of India left behind is palpable, but the polemic in this poem is cleverly disguised; hidden under its surface. Through its narrative in a free-flowing style, not limited by a rhyme scheme or clear metrical patterns, Bhatt brings the vast scale of this geopolitical crisis – and human tragedy – down to an intimate, domestic scale. It becomes almost a pastoral scene in the garden with the solitary female figure 'listening' beneath 'the shadows cast by the neem trees', but far from an idyll, the space becomes enclosing, trapping, confining – limiting. By switching so clearly from the 'then' to the 'now', Bhatt seems to draw a line under the past, and the horrific events of partition, but is ultimately unable to escape them. They dominate the physical spaces of the present – as much in 'her kitchen' as on the page – and lead to a questioning exasperation that asks tough and challenging questions both of patriarchal power and, most importantly, of the murky business of colonialism and its legacy.

Partition squeezed:

THEN – GARDEN – CRIES – STRANDED – FELT – NEW – AUNT – STATION – FOOD – AFRAID – NOT – STOOD – DIFFERENT – SHADOWS – CONSOLATION – WISHED – COURAGE – EACH – PEOPLE – NOW – ME – KITCHEN – INDIA – BUT – OLDER – ALWAYS – WISH – GAVE – STATION – STILL – GUILT – ASKS – WHO – LET – NOTHING – GEOGRAPHY – DIVIDE

'A poem is as clear as a drink of water, as rigorous [and as rare] as an honest judge, as packed full of meaning as a ripe apple is packed with white flesh.'

THEO DORGAN

A sonnet of revision activities

1. Reverse millionaire: 10,000 points if students can guess the poem just from one word from it. You can vary the difficulty as much as you like. For example, 'doomed', from Owen's poem would be fairly easily identifiable whereas 'shires' would be more difficult. 1000 points if students can name the poem from a single phrase or image – 'portion out the stars and dates'. 100 points for a single line. 10 points for recognising the poem from a stanza. Play individually or in teams.

2. Research the poet. Find one sentence about them that you think sheds light on their poem in the anthology. Compare with your classmates. Or find a couple more lines or a stanza by a poet and see if others can recognise the writer from their lines.

3. Write a cento based on one or more of the poems. A cento is a poem constructed from lines from other poems. Difficult, creative, but also fun, perhaps.

4. Read 3 or 4 other poems by one of the poets. Write a pastiche. See if classmates can recognise the poet you're imitating.

5. Write the introduction for a critical guide on the poems aimed at next year's yr. 10 class.

6. Use the poet Glynn Maxwell's typology of poems to arrange the poems into separate groups. In his excellent book, *On Poetry*, Maxwell suggests poems have four dominant aspects, which he calls solar, lunar, musical and visual. A solar poem hits home, is immediately striking. A lunar poem, by contrast, is more mysterious and might not give up its meanings so easily. Ideally a lunar poem will haunt your imagination. Written mainly for the ear, a musical poem focuses on the sounds of language, rather than the meanings. Think of Lewis Carroll's

Jabberwocky. A visual poem is self-conscious about how it looks to the eye. Concrete poems are the ultimate visual poems. According to Maxwell, the very best poems are strong in each dimension. Try applying this test to each poem. Which ones come out on top?

7. Maxwell also recommends conceptualising the context in which the words of the poem are created or spoken. Which poems would suit being read around a camp fire? Which would be better declaimed from the top of a tall building? Which might you imagine on a stage? Which ones are more like conversation overheard? Which are the easiest and which the most difficult to place?

8. Mr Maxwell is a fund of interesting ideas. He suggests all poems dramatise a battle between the forces of whiteness and blackness, nothingness and somethingness, sound and silence, life and death. In each poem, what is the dynamic between whiteness and blackness? Which appears to have the upper hand?

9. Still thinking in terms of evaluation, consider the winnowing effect of time. Which of the modern poems in the anthology do you think might be still in school poetry anthologies in 20, a 100 or 200 years? Why?

10. Give yourself only the first and last line of one of the poems. Without peeking at the original, try to fill in the middle. Easy level: write in prose. Expert level: attempt verse.

11. According to Russian Formalist critics, poetry performs a 'controlled explosion on ordinary language'. What evidence can you find in this selection of controlled linguistic detonations?

12. A famous musician once said that though he wasn't the best at playing all the notes, nobody played the silences better. In Japanese garden water features the sound of a water drop is designed to make us notice the silence around it. Try reading one of the poems in the light of these

comments, focusing on the use of white space, caesuras, punctuation – all the devices that create the silence on which the noise of the poem rests.

13. In *Notes on the Art of Poetry*, Dylan Thomas wrote that 'the best craftsmanship always leaves holes and gaps in the works of the poem so that something that is not in the poem can creep, crawl, flash or thunder in'. Examine a poem in the light of this comment, looking for its holes and gaps. If you discover these, what 'creeps', 'crawls' or 'flashes' in to fill them?

14. Different types of poems conceive the purpose of poetry differently. Broadly speaking Augustan poets of the eighteenth century aimed to impress their readers with the wit of their ideas and the elegance of the expression. In contrast, Romantic poets wished to move their readers' hearts. Characteristically Victorian poets aimed to teach the readers some kind of moral principle or example. Self-involved, avant-garde Modernists weren't overly bothered about finding, never mind pleasing, a general audience. What impact do the OCR anthology poems seek to have? Do they aim to amuse, appeal to the heart, teach us something? Are they like soliloquies – the overheard inner workings of thinking – or more like speeches or mini-plays? Try placing each poem somewhere on the following continuums. Then create a few continuums of your own. As ever, comparison with your classmates will prove illuminating.

Emotional...intellectual
Feelings..ideas
Internal..external
Contemplative..rhetorical
Open..guarded
Experimental..conventional

130

Terminology task

The following is a list of poetry terminology and short definitions of the terms. Unfortunately, cruel, malicious individuals (i.e. us) have scrambled them up. Your task is to unscramble the list, matching each term to the correct definition. Good luck!

Term	Definition
Imagery	Vowel rhyme, e.g. 'bat' and 'lag'
Metre	An implicit comparison in which one thing is said to be another
Rhythm	
Simile	Description in poetry
Metaphor	A conventional metaphor, such as a 'dove' for peace
Symbol	A metrical foot comprising an unstressed followed by a stressed beat
Iambic	
Pentameter	A line with five beats
Enjambment	Description in poetry using metaphor, simile or personification
Caesura	
Dramatic monologue	A repeated pattern of ordered sound
Figurative imagery	An explicit comparison of two things, using 'like' or 'as'
Onomatopoeia	Words, or combinations of words, whose sounds mimic their meaning
Lyric	
Adjective	Words in a line starting with the same letter or sound
Alliteration	A strong break in a line, usually signalled by punctuation
Ballad	A regular pattern of beats in each line
Sonnet	A narrative poem with an alternating four and three beat line
Assonance	
Sensory imagery	A word that describes a noun
Quatrain	A 14-line poem following several possible rhyme schemes
Diction	When a sentence steps over the end of a line and continues into the next line or stanza
Personification	
	Description that uses the senses
	A four-line stanza
	Inanimate objects given human characteristics
	A poem written in the voice of a character
	A poem written in the first person, focusing on the emotional experience of the narrator
	A term to describe the vocabulary used in a poem.

GLOSSARY

ALLITERATION – the repetition of consonants at the start of neighbouring words in a line

ANAPAEST - a three beat pattern of syllables, unstress, unstress, stress. E.g. 'on the moon', 'to the coast', 'anapaest'

ANTITHESIS - the use of balanced opposites

APOSTROPHE – a figure of speech addressing a person, object or idea

ASSONANCE – vowel rhyme, e.g. sod and block

BLANK VERSE – unrhymed lines of iambic pentameter

BLAZON – a male lover describing the parts of his beloved

CADENCE – the rise of fall of sounds in a line of poetry

CAESURA – a distinct break in a poetic line, usually marked by punctuation

COMPLAINT – a type of love poem concerned with loss and mourning

CONCEIT – an extended metaphor

CONSONANCE – rhyme based on consonants only, e.g. book and back

COUPLET – a two-line stanza, conventionally rhyming

DACTYL – the reverse pattern to the anapaest; stress, unstress, unstress. E.g. 'Strong as a'

DRAMATIC MONOLOGUE – a poem written in the voice of a distinct character

ELEGY – a poem in mourning for someone dead

END-RHYME – rhyming words at the end of a line

END-STOPPED – the opposite of enjambment; i.e. when the sentence and the poetic line stop at the same point

ENJAMBMENT – where sentences run over the end of lines and stanzas

FIGURATIVE LANGUAGE – language that is not literal, but employs figures of speech, such as metaphor, simile and personification

FEMININE RHYME – a rhyme that ends with an unstressed syllable or unstressed syllables.

FREE VERSE – poetry without metre or a regular, set form

GOTHIC – a style of literature characterised by psychological horror, dark deeds and uncanny events

HEROIC COUPLETS – pairs of rhymed lines in iambic pentameter

HYPERBOLE – extreme exaggeration

IAMBIC – a metrical pattern of a weak followed by a strong stress, ti-TUM, like a heart beat

IMAGERY – the umbrella term for description in poetry. Sensory imagery refers to descriptions that appeal to sight, sound and so forth; figurative imagery refers to the use of devices such as metaphor, simile and personification

JUXTAPOSITION – two things placed together to create a stark contrast

LYRIC – an emotional, personal poem usually with a first-person speaker

MASCULINE RHYME – an end rhyme on a strong syllable

METAPHOR – an implicit comparison in which one thing is said to be another

METAPHYSICAL – a type of poetry characterised by wit and extended metaphors

METRE – the regular pattern organising sound and rhythm in a poem

MOTIF – a repeated image or pattern of language, often carrying thematic significance

OCTET OR OCTAVE – the opening eight lines of a sonnet

ONOMATOPOEIA – bang, crash, wallop

PENTAMETER – a poetic line consisting of five beats

PERSONIFICATION – giving human characteristics to inanimate things

PLOSIVE – a type of alliteration using 'p' and 'b' sounds

QUATRAIN – a four-line stanza

REFRAIN – a line or lines repeated like a chorus

ROMANTIC – A type of poetry characterised by a love of nature, by strong emotion and heightened tone

SESTET – the last six lines in a sonnet

SIMILE – an explicit comparison of two different things

SONNET – a form of poetry with fourteen lines and a variety of possible set rhyme patterns

SPONDEE – two strong stresses together in a line of poetry

STANZA – the technical name for a verse

SYMBOL – something that stands in for something else. Often a concrete representation of an idea.

SYNTAX – the word order in a sentence. doesn't Without sense English syntax make. Syntax is crucial to sense: For example, though it uses all the same words, 'the man eats the fish' is not the same as 'the fish eats the man'

TERCET – a three-line stanza

TETRAMETER – a line of poetry consisting of four beats

TROCHEE – the opposite of an iamb; stress, unstress, strong, weak.

VILLANELLE – a complex interlocking verse form in which lines are recycled

VOLTA – the 'turn' in a sonnet from the octave to the sestet

Recommended reading

Atherton, C., Green, A & Snapper, G. Teaching English Literature 16-19. NATE, 2013

Bowen et al. The Art of Poetry, vol.1-14. Peripeteia Press, 2015-17

Brinton, I. Contemporary Poetry. CUP, 2009

Eagleton, T. How to Read a Poem. Wiley & Sons, 2006

Fry, S. The Ode Less Travelled. Arrow, 2007

Hamilton, I. & Noel-Todd, J. Oxford Companion to Modern Poetry, OUP, 2014

Herbert, W. & Hollis, M. Strong Words. Bloodaxe, 2000

Howarth, P. The Cambridge Introduction to Modernist Poetry. CUP, 2012

Hurley, M. & O'Neill, M. Poetic Form, An Introduction. CUP, 2012

Meally, M. & Bowen, N. The Art of Writing English Literature Essays, Peripeteia Press, 2014

Maxwell, G. On Poetry. Oberon Masters, 2012

Padel, R. 52 Ways of Looking at a Poem. Vintage, 2004

Padel, R. The Poem and the Journey. Vintage, 2008

Paulin, T. The Secret Life of Poems. Faber & Faber, 2011

Schmidt, M. Lives of the Poets, Orion, 1998

Wolosky, S. The Art of Poetry: How to Read a Poem. OUP, 2008.

About the authors

Head of English and freelance writer, Neil Bowen has a Masters Degree in Literature & Education from Cambridge University and is a member of Ofqual's experts panel for English. He is the author of *The Art of Writing English Essays for GCSE*, co-author of *The Art of Writing English Essays for A-level and Beyond* and of *The Art of Poetry* series. Neil runs the peripeteia project, bridging the gap between A-level and degree level English courses: www.peripeteia.webs.com.

Johanna Harrison completed a degree in English Literature at Regent's Park College, Oxford University. A professional opera singer and tutor in English, she is now studying music in London.

After completing an English Literature degree at Cambridge University, Jack May began a career in journalism and currently he is working as a sub-editor for a national newspaper.

Michael Meally is an Irish English teacher with degrees in Engineering and English Literature and a MA in American Literature. He is the co-author of *The Art of Writing English Literature Essays for A-level and Beyond* and of *The Art of Poetry critical guides*. Michael also writes regularly for the English & Media Centre magazine.

Printed in Great Britain
by Amazon